六安
包種

福港室茶莊

福港室茶莊

狀元梅花水片

狀元梅花水片

金圓
貢品烏龍

鐵觀音寄種

荷花水片

我國飲茶的起源和利用茶葉的發現，是世界上最早的。茶葉作為「貢品」，傳說在西周初期，我國西南一帶部落已有。如果花西周以前，即開始飲用的時間，前後相距竟達千餘年之久。其實，我國飲茶開始的年代，無論說是秦漢或是春秋，都說得太遲。更不消說是在晉代了。根據記載，周武王伐紂後，巴蜀等西南小國曾以所產之茶葉作「貢品」。這可說一種比較珍貴的飲料。到了兩晉、南北朝，產茶漸多，傳播日廣，關於飲茶的記載也日益增多。

茶葉作為相當普遍的飲料，應是在西晉以前，我國江南一帶，哪裡能夠「課童茶蘇」呢？可以想見，我國飲茶就相當普遍了。在西晉以前，中國廣大地區還是把茶葉作為一種比較珍貴的飲料。

到了唐代，南北各省、飲茶逐漸向中、下游推進，這時發展為日常性的飲料，有許多文獻的記載。

茶的起源和利用茶葉。因沒有過去長期積累下來的茶樹栽培和製茶經驗。如果沒有人群眾對茶葉的消費需求，哪裡能夠製茶的技藝。

茶，在我國被人們利用，發現這種綠葉真奇怪，一直到肚子裡，就從上到下，從下到上，到處流動洗滌，好似把胃腸洗滌得乾乾淨淨。神農成年累月地爬山涉水，常要經過一段漫長的歲月，全靠茶來解毒。茶和其他植物一樣，從發現到利用，需要經過一段漫長的歲月。當原始人類發現茶葉對人體有醫療效用，於是對茶及其以後，對茶葉的歲月，就開始注意和重視起來。據古籍記載，茶葉最初只作藥用。到了春秋時代，已經提到用茶葉作專門作為飲料的記載。有許多文獻的記錄，有的認為，秦人取蜀（四川），而時發展成為飲料。有定論。有的認為茶和茶始於秦漢時，即產和茶始於秦漢時，作者說飲茶家說紛紜，對茶葉的因此，對茶葉。

造成了人口的大遷徙。特別是秦統一中國以後，促進了經濟和文化的交流，四川、雲南一帶的茶樹栽培、茶葉加工及飲用方法，開始向當時的經濟、政治、文化中心陝西、河南等地傳播，這是陝西、河南成為北方古老茶日相仿佛的茶肆。只要投錢，隨時都可以取飲。據唐人封演《封氏聞見記》記載：開元（公元七一三至七四一年）

六安
包種
華投春，隱隱

福若堂茶莊

狀元梅花水片

茗堂
貴賓光顧此票另有記

茶葉作為「貢品」。如果在西周初期，我國西南一帶部落已經開始的年代，都說得太遲，更不消說是秦漢或是春秋，對茶葉始飲的時間，前後各種相距甚達千餘年之久。其實，我國飲茶開始的年代，無論說是秦漢或是春秋，都說得太遲。根據記載，巴蜀等西南一帶曾以所產達千餘年之久。其實，我國飲茶有過去長期積累下來的茶樹栽培和製茶經驗。如果沒有人民對茶葉的消費需求，哪裡能夠「課童茶葉就相當普遍了。在西晉以前，中國廣大地區還是把茶始於三國。有人根據西晉時張載有「芳茶冠六清，溢味播九區」之句，有人根據西晉時張載《登成都樓詩》中有「芳茶（茶字古作茶）冠六清，溢味播九區」之句，

福若堂茶莊

狀元梅花水片

茗堂
福開張檢提
茶葉加芽揉造細嫩
發行
香港中環遮打道太子行
商場二百二十一室

茶葉作為珍貴的貢品，由此可以推想到西漢以前，茶葉已在晉代了。較珍貴的飲茶葉作為一種比較珍貴的飲料。到了兩晉、南北朝，產茶漸多，傳播日廣，關於飲茶的記載也日益增多。據《晉書》記載，敦煌人單道開是西晉末年中興書》有一段與吳太守陸納結生活儉樸，以茶果待客的故事：王濛是西晉時四川賓中的一位儒生，到成都的有之宗之宗女文成公主，一是唐太宗之宗女文成公主，文化與飲茶的風尚從內地輸入西藏。尼泊爾輸入西藏，文化與飲茶的風尚更進一步結合，導致以後在西藏喇嘛寺中盛大茶會的出現。唐代國人民主要的消費品。唐代

福若堂茶莊

狀元梅花水片

茗堂
福開張檢提
茶葉加芽揉造細嫩
發行
香港中環遮打道太子行
商場二百二十一室

山縣約十市里，為漢代即今四川彭山縣東，距彭「武陽買茶」，「烹茶盡具」兩句。武陽定便了每天從事務役，其中涉及茶的有所立契約就是王褒所寫的《僮約》。在《僮約》中規「烹茶盡具」、「武陽買茶」。王褒所寫的《僮約》，便了去沽酒，便了老婢，時常要寡婦楊氏的家便了去沽酒，茶的起源距今當有三、四千年，便居在他亡友的妻子楊惠家裡。

金圓
貢品烏龍

「陸納為吳興太守時，衛將軍謝安欲詣納，
「陸納為吳興太守時，衛將軍謝安欲詣納，
納兄子俶，怪納無所備，不敢問之，乃私
蓄十數人饌，安既至，納所設唯茶果而已，
俶遂陳盛饌，珍羞畢俱，及安去，納杖俶
四十，云：『汝既不能光益叔父，奈何穢吾
素業。』」《南濟書》記載：齊
武帝臨崩前在一道詔書上
寫道：「我靈上慎勿以牲
為祭。唯設餅果、茶飲、
乾飯、酒脯而已。天下貴賤，咸同此制。」

茶始於三國。曾在宴會上密賜茶茗代酒，於是有人認為茶曾在宴會上密賜茶茗代酒。三國時，吳末帝孫皓因大臣韋曜酒量太又據史料記載，漢室都一種飲料了。又據史料記載，漢王曾在江蘇宜興茶嶺「課童藝茶」。浙江臨海蓋竹山有仙翁茶嶺，漢朝名士江蘇宜興茶嶺「課童藝茶」。

華投春，隱隱
到京南各省。漢代
的史料逐漸增多。漢代
到京南各省。漢代
以後，記載茶事
如西漢揚雄《蜀
茶之句子：「百
芬芳，蔓茶茇郁，翠茶青黃」。在《趙飛燕別傳》中，有一段關於漢代飲茶的記載：漢成帝崩，「后（即帝后）寢驚啼甚久，侍者呼問，方覺，乃言曰：適吾夢中見帝，帝命吾坐，賜吾坐，帝命進茶。左右奏帝，后向日侍帝不謹，不合啜此茶。」

武陽縣約十市里
即今四川彭山縣

鐵觀音家

福茗堂
香港中環遮打道太子行
商場二百二十一室
本號在太子行
開張檢提
茶葉加芽揉造細嫩
發行

山東、河北的部份地區，直至當時的首都長安。「城市多開店鋪，煎茶賣之，不問道俗，投錢取飲，其茶自江淮而來，舟車相繼，所在山積，色額甚多。」同書又說：「古人亦飲茶耳，但不如今人溺之甚，窮日盡夜，殆成風俗。」

狀元梅花水片

茗堂
福開張檢提
茶葉加芽揉造細嫩
發行
香港中環遮打道太子行
商場二百二十一室

六安
包種

茶稅也開始徵收了。到了宋代，茶已發展為交換西北邊前月浮梁買茶去」之句。唐德宗貞元九年（公元七九三年），茶稅也開始徵收了。到了宋代有「商人重利輕別離，前月浮梁買茶去」之句。白居易《琵琶行》中以所以浮梁、湖州都是著名的茶葉集散地。現今茶區基本相同。當時茶葉產量以江淮一帶較多。浙江、四川、雲南、廣西、貴州等地，產現今茶區，河南、廣東、福建、安徽、產湖北、四川、雲南、浙江、安徽、產江蘇、廣及江蘇、浙江、安徽、產國人民主要的消費品。唐代

金圓
貢品烏龍

西北邊土特產的主要商品。所以，茶已開始設立了茶市。這時茶已發展到交換西北邊在西北邊疆區也設立了茶市。這時茶已發展為交換西北邊年），茶稅也開始徵收了。到了宋代，不僅在內地，即民，現在已成為綠茶的嗜好者，而軟使徒也成為嗜好飲茶的居民多數信奉伊，北非摩洛哥、突尼斯、阿爾及利亞等地，原因之一是生活於戒律的國家後來，由陸上商路經西伯利亞源源運往俄國，並由此轉銷歐洲，使斯拉夫族也成為嗜好飲茶的民族。茶的傳播幾乎遍及全球。

鐵觀音家

普洱

論述。在唐代，南北城鎮已出現了與今日相仿佛的茶肆。反映在西漢時期，茶已成為皇室中的一種飲料了。又據史料記載，漢王往年回紇入。可知唐時飲茶之風，已由南方傳播到黃河北岸，並且遠傳到塞外西北各地。不但如此，就是原來只飲酪漿，並以茶飲為恥事的少數民族，一旦領略了飲茶的奇特風味，也很快染上飲茶嗜好。茶遂漸成為他們日常生活中不可缺少的必需品。據唐朝李肇著的《國史補》記載：唐朝有使者叫常魯公，到了西番，烹茶帳中。贊普問他著什麼，常魯公說：「滌煩療渴之所謂茶。」贊普說，我這裡也有。於是叫人拿出來指着說：「此壽州者，此舒州者，此顧渚者，此蘄門者，此昌明者，此澠湖者。」可見唐時飲茶風氣之盛，連新疆、西藏一帶的王公貴族家裡都貯備各色名茶了。還值得一提的是，唐代飲茶傳播到西藏，是同文成公主分不開的。吐蕃的松贊干布娶普有兩個王妃，一是唐太宗之宗女文成公主，一是尼泊爾的赤尊公主，文成公主從內地輸入西藏。於是，宗教從尼泊爾輸入西藏，文化與飲茶風尚從內地輸入西藏，導致以後在西藏喇嘛寺中盛大茶會的出現。茶已成為全國人民主要的消費品了。

福茗堂

狀元梅花水片

茗堂
福開張檢提
茶葉加芽揉造細嫩
發行
香港中環遮打道太子行
商場二百二十一室

中從

到了明萬曆四十六年（公元一六一八年），我國正式將中國茶葉首次輸往歐洲。明隆慶元年（公一五六七年），有兩位俄國人飲用茶的記載。茶葉從陸路輸出歐洲和亞洲其它地區的歷史也很長遠。早在五世紀的南北朝時，土耳其已有茶葉輸入。後來傳到波斯、阿拉伯等地。十七世紀初期，波斯帝國回國內，而茶葉傳入伊雍正年間，美國消費量最多的茶產城鎮和鄉村。茶葉在陸路輸出歐洲和亞洲其它地區的歷史也很長遠。到了

一五六七年
國
到波斯、阿拉伯等地
到波斯、阿拉伯等地
則在明萬曆四十六年（公元一六一八年）

茗堂
福開張檢提
茶葉加芽揉造細嫩
發行
香港中環遮打道太子行
商場二百二十一室

最初提到我國茶葉的是明世宗嘉靖二十八年（公元一五四九年）威尼斯著名作家拉馬司沃所著的《中國茶》和《出海與旅行記》兩書。葡萄牙傳教士克魯茲神父是在中國傳播及飲茶方法等知識傳入歐洲。明神宗萬曆三十五年（公元一六〇七年），荷蘭海船最初將茶從澳門運販往荷蘭，這是歐洲直接販銷往歐洲來澳門販茶運往歐洲，這是歐洲直接運銷往歐洲的最早記錄。以後，茶葉就成為荷蘭最時髦的飲料。由於荷蘭人的宣傳，飲茶之風波及到英、法等國。英國一個名叫威茲成的船長喜程牽引去英國，首次從中國運去茶葉，成了英六三七年，船隊東行，首次從中國直接運去茶葉。到荷蘭人和英國人都喊香，荷蘭人和英國人都視茶最初當作珍貴的禮品餽送給歐洲時，茶最初當作珍貴的禮品，當茶最初價格最昂貴。當茶最初輸入歐洲時，茶最初。隨着茶葉輸入量的不斷增加。隨着茶葉輸入量的不斷品。隨着茶葉輸入量的不斷價格逐漸下降，成為家喻的飲料。後來，英國人喝界上最大的消費國。到了

一六三七年
一六六二年
三十五年（公元一六〇七年）

普洱
六安
包種

福茗堂
香港中環遮打道太子行
商場二百二十一室
本號在太子行
開張檢提
茶葉加芽揉造細嫩
發行

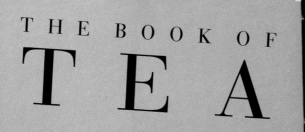

THE BOOK OF
TEA

PREFACE
BY ANTHONY BURGESS

ARTISTIC DIRECTION
MARC WALTER

TRANSLATED
BY DEKE DUSINBERRE

Flammarion

Editorial Direction
GHISLAINE BAVOILLOT

Artistic Direction
MARC WALTER

Copyediting
JULIE GASKILL

Picture Research
SABINE ARQUÉ
NADINE BEAUTHÉAC

Map
LÉONIE SCHLOSSER

Typesetting
OCTAVO ÉDITIONS

Photoengraving
COLOURSCAN FRANCE

ISBN : 2-08-013533-3

Printed in Italy

N° d'édition : 0511

Dépôt légal : October 1992

CONTENTS

◆ PREFACE ◆

by Anthony Burgess

Samuel Pepys, the diarist of the reign of Charles II, who came to the British throne in 1660, writes of having drunk "tee (a China drinke) of which I had never drank before." He does not say whether he liked it or not. There was at first some dissension as to its preparation. It could be either too strong or too weak. Should it be sweetened or not? In the eighteenth century the greatest tea drinker of all time established the way the British were to drink it. This was Dr. Samuel Johnson, the lexicographer who created his huge English Dictionary single-handed, no doubt under the stimulation of tea. His teapot held two litres. He took it strong, the bite of the tannin being allayed with a little milk, adding sugar in little lumps. At the house of a distinguished lady, he kept passing his cup for more and more, until he had ingested thirty-two cups. The lady said: "Dr. Johnson, you drink too much tea." Johnson said "Madam, you are insolent." Clearly, the very British institution of the tea party, or what the French call *le five o'clock*, had been established by this time. It still goes on. Tea has become not merely the name of a beverage but the name of a meal. Sandwiches and cakes accompany the cheerful cups. In the north of England, where the meal is called "high tea," there are lamb chops and fried potatoes as well. The tea is, so to speak, swamped by the circumambient food. But it is still there, hot, strong and copious.

The first British tea drinkers got their leaf from China. But the stronger and less delicate varieties from India and Ceylon have tended to dominate the market (whose centre is Mincing Lane, in the heart of that part of London known as the

Wry humor and the love of tea are both quintessentially English characteristics. On average, the English drink six cups per day per person, rivaling the Chinese as the world's heaviest consumers of tea. *Opposite:* A chambermaid in Cambridge in 1939, during the ritual tea break that punctuated the working day.

City). China tea is for exquisite people like Oscar Wilde; his compatriots, still living in Ireland, demand the brutal overstewed Indian variety. The Irish taste in tea is also the taste of the British working class. Most tea-addicts of humble origins, such as myself, will opt for Twining's Irish Breakfast Tea—the leaf or the sachet—with Twining's Darjeeling as a close competitor. The drawing rooms of the ruling class prefer the perfume of Earl Gray or Lapsang. The lower orders, given tea in a pot with thimble-sized cups in a Chinese restaurant, accept the exotic bestowal but do not take it seriously. After the meal, they go home and brew some real, meaning Indian or Ceylon, tea. The Russian way, passed on to the immigrant Jews of Britain, is unacceptable to the British gentile on two counts—there is no milk, and the beverage is served in a glass. But it is strong (Russian Caravan tea has none of the fragile allure of the Chinese variety) and it is sweetened with a spoonful of jam. But a *stakan chai*—a glass of tea—is a frightening anomaly. Tea is not tea to the British unless it is poured into a cup.

A cup, yes, but there is a class division centred on what precisely is meant by a cup. The upper class have the most exquisite china, but the tea poured into it is a mere mouthful. A mug—a much larger cup with no saucer—is the lower-class receptacle. The class division was made almost blatantly clear in World War II, when the commissioned officers took their tea in upper-class china in the officers' mess, while the rest of the army was issued with a mug that held half a litre of tea brewed coarsely in a bucket (flavoured with cigarette ash or even rhinoid mucus). The Asterix cartoon about the tea-maddened Britons was a kind of retrospective prophecy: Britain could not have fought either of the two major wars of our century without tea.

The really important beverage division concerns itself with tea and coffee. Tea versus coffee? In the eighteenth century, London had its coffee houses, where hot chocolate was also served. There were no tea houses: these were an oriental affectation. Tea was for home consumption. Coffee is always difficult to brew, and few British homes offer a good cup of it.

"It is proper both for Winter and Summer, preserving in perfect health until extreme old age, it maketh the body active and lusty . . . it removeth lassitude and cleanseth acrid humours. . . ." Thus Thomas Garraway praised the virtues of tea in the mid-seventeenth century. Garraway was the first to import the magic potion from China and sell it in England. *Above:* In the French comic book series *Asterix*, the heroic Gaul of the title concocts this "barbarous" potion for a Breton warrior, who comments that the recipe seems easy enough. *Opposite:* A portable tea trolley at Wimbledon on 21 June 1937 enables tennis fans who have lined up in front of ticket windows since dawn to rid themselves of "lassitude."

Instant coffee is served with a certain gloom: no one really likes it, but the making of the real thing is beyond the powers of British home technology. Coffee-making is for professionals, and the professionals made it in the eighteenth-century coffee houses. Some of these were not only famous for their brew: they were the centres of political and literary argument, like Wills's. Lloyd's coffee house, which purveyed the latest shipping news as one of its amenities, became the greatest insurance centre in the world. Tea has never been associated with public life. It is too domestic. It is sometimes, as for instance by Ian Fleming's creation James Bond, considered a drink for women. Coffee, like the brandy that accompanies it, is for men. The working class begs to differ.

That there is a kind of enmity between tea and coffee is supposed to be illustrated by the revolt of the American colonies from British rule. The New England Americans drank tea like their cousins in the homeland, but they resented the heavy tax imposed on it by the government in London. Hence the Boston Tea Party, in which patriotic Americans, dressed as Mohawk Indians, hurled whole tons of the imported leaf into Boston harbour. This led to the War of Independence and the tradition of American coffee-drinking in imitation of the French. The Americans, just like the French, do not know how to make tea. One of Graham Greene's characters knows that he is in Paris when he sees a man at an open-air café dipping a teabag into tepid water, holding it by its stringy tail like a mouse. The Americans have forgotten the art they brought over from Britain: they too are great teabag-dippers.

In American hotels, from Vermont to Florida, I have pleaded with waiters and waitresses for strong tea. I always end up with warm water and a sachet of Earl Gray. At a Holiday Inn I gave detailed instructions. Take one of those coffee jugs. Place in it six bags of Lipton's or Twining's Indian or Ceylon. Pour on boiling water. Bring it to me. This was, in a manner, done for me in Minneapolis. The only trouble was that the six bags had been stewed in warm coffee. A coffee jug was for coffee; ergo, coffee had to be in it. I tend now to travel through the United States with my own half-litre mug and electric kettle. This is considered very British.

Before I go further, it would be in order for me to state here how precisely tea ought to be prepared. First, you must have a capacious teapot. Then you must have a kettle. Boil your water and at the

In England, establishments that serve tea have always been considered ideal meeting places for people from all walks of life. The original coffee houses (Thomas Twining opened one that also served tea as early as 1706) evolved into tea gardens and eventually into tea rooms. Such places are increasingly rare, unfortunately, and in present-day London, afternoon tea is served mainly in the grand hotels. *Opposite:* Two enlisted soldiers on leave enjoy afternoon tea at a Lyons Corner House on Coventry Street in 1926.

same time heat your teapot. It is unwise to heat it by swilling warm water around in it: it will be difficult to swill all of this out, and thus the inside of the teapot will be wet. It must be perfectly dry. Place the teapot in an inch or so of very hot water; when its external bottom is hot enough to make the hand uncomfortable, its internal bottom is hot enough for tea. Place into the warmed pot, according to the tradition, one teaspoonful for each drinker and an extra teaspoonful as a gift for the pot. You may, of course, increase these doses according to taste or, more accurately, to habituation. I substitute a dessert spoon for a teaspoon. Pour on boiling water from the kettle. Stir the infusion gently. Place the lid on the pot and leave it for five minutes. Then pour into cup or mug.

If you take milk with your tea—no more than a minute amount to soften the impact of the tannin content—you must decide which faction to belong to—the one that puts the milk into the cup before pouring the tea, or the school that drips milk in while the tea lies black and

steaming. I do not think it makes very much difference: it is one of these very British controversies which keep off the *tedium vitae*. You may then add sugar, but this is frowned upon by many tea-drinking experts. The late George Orwell was one of these. He published an essay, rather less well-known than his *Nineteen Eighty-Four* (one of the horrors of which seems to be a total absence of tea, though not gin), whose title is "A Nice Cup of Tea." In it he says that the addition of sugar kills the taste of the tea. He also says that the older one grows the stronger one prefers one's tea. One of the few good qualities he found in Britain's wartime Ministry of Food was its willingness to grant a larger ration of tea to citizens over 65 (60 if they were women) than to the younger and unseasoned.

Tea, though so much a feature of the British scene, is a highly exotic substance. Nazi U-boats sank a great many of the merchant vessels bringing food to British shores, especially in the Atlantic, but exiguous imports of tea came in from India

In Great Britain, as in many other places, taking tea is often a subtle and refined occasion that requires a small measure of artistry. To savor tea time fully, one must know how to take the time to relax, how to leave daily cares behind and appreciate the simple pleasures of the moment. It is thus associated with luxury, whatever the circumstances, and is often conducive to wit and good humor, particularly among the English. *Above:* A silkscreen by Floc'h and Rivière, the *Tea Tanic*, produced in conjunction with their comic book, *A la Recherche de Sir Malcolm. Opposite:* On the deck of a transatlantic liner in the 1920s.

and Ceylon: the Japanese naval force was busy in the Pacific but not so much in the Indian Ocean, and the British Navy kept the tea-lines open in the Red Sea and the Mediterranean. Without tea Britain could not have fought the war. A novel by Len Deighton called *SS-GB* presents an imaginary England under the heel of the Germans from 1940 on (an analogue of the French situation). There is tea available for the enslaved British, but it is in a powdered form and its flavour is of *ersatz* lemon. That is the way the Nazi occupying troops prefer it. Deighton's characters suffer but do not revolt. Here the book is less than plausible. Without real tea the enslaved British would have risked the perils of insurrection. I do not exaggerate. We cannot do without it.

It is, if you wish, a drug, though the drop of milk relates it to our mother's wholesome breasts. Dr. Johnson's biographer, James Boswell, feared that the Grand Cham's perpetual consumption of strong tea might injure his nerves. But, though the tannin may, in some feeble instances, harm the digestive system, it will do so far less than will the French wine so many of us are abandoning. For wine is increasingly charged with tannin. There is still a British superstition that to drink strong tea with a grilled steak, or the Sunday slices of roast beef, literally tans the meat and turns it to leather. This is a small price to pay for the enlivening effect of a morning, mid-morning, lunchtime, afternoon, evening, late evening, and midnight pot of tea. I say pot advisedly, and I imply tea in the leaf, not the sachet. For there are rumours that the paper of the teabag is not altogether healthy; there is an obscure reaction between the chemical substances in the leaf and its dioxinsoaked container which brings on some disease or other. But the teabag, however convenient, was always, anyway, a travesty of the loaded spoon and its aromatic heap of the real thing.

Teabags tend to be preferred these days because the disposal of the infused, spent, soggy tea leaves in the cold pot is difficult. You cannot swill them down the kitchen sink without risking the clogging of the drains. To pour them into the toilet and flush them down lends an excremental flavour to what has been a civilised potation. Hens like them mixed with old bread, but few people keep hens. You can spread them lightly on the floor and sweep them away along with the dust they attract. You can keep them in the teapot and bring them back to life with boiling water, but

In 1942, Churchill claimed that tea was more important to his soldiers than ammunition. All the English agreed that their morale would not have withstood the bombing, nor would their army have defeated the Afrika Korps, if they had been deprived of their national beverage. Tea was the ultimate British weapon during World War II, for it was not only a comfort but also a rare pleasure, and therefore a powerful symbol of freedom. *Opposite:* An example of the family shelters that civil defense organizations designed and promoted among the civilian population.

their vitality has vanished and you are drinking a ghost. They are a nuisance when their usefulness is past, just like people. But to prefer teabags to real tea is to exalt the shadow over the substance.

The substance remains so magical that it is strange that it has been so little celebrated in the arts. It was a Frenchman, Maurice Ravel, who celebrated *le five o'clock* in a jazzy dance in *L'Enfant et les sortilèges*, but no Englishman has produced a musical work on tea analogous to Bach's *Coffee Cantata*. A member of parliament, A. P. Herbert, wrote a vapid song with the refrain "A Nice Cup of Tea" (a cup of tea is always "nice" in England, just as a beefsteak is always *una bella bistecca* in Italy). The poet William Cowper praised "the cups that cheer but not inebriate." But there the literature of tea comes to an end. I doubt if there is an English book devoted to tea. Here, however, is a French one. Perhaps tea is so woven into the stomach linings of the British that they cannot view it in either a scholarly or an aesthetic manner. It is a fact of British life, like breathing.

A nice cup of tea taken to delightful excess. *Above:* "The largest teapot in the world," displayed at the 1938 Empire Exhibition, boasted a two-gallon capacity. *Opposite:* On a sweltering summer day in 1947, typists from the City (London's business district) take a tea break at the Endell Street pool.

· TEA ·

GARDENS

Alain Stella

To find out what all of the world's finest tea gardens—from the Far East to West Africa—have in common, stroll through one at nightfall. At this hour, the gardens resemble one another. They are brushed by the same thick clouds and cool mountain air, and cleansed by the same rain. They all proffer a concert of rainfall on leaves, of swollen torrents and cascades, and they all exude the same odors of warm, moist earth. For wherever it is cultivated, tea will impart its highly sought, subtle fragrances only if grown in a wet and temperate climate—long sunny days followed by rainy nights and pure mountain breezes.

It is only at daybreak, when the first birds break into song and clouds scatter beyond the horizon or nestle low in the valleys, when the sun's rays transform the mist into a glittery dew on the leaves, that the infinite variety of tea gardens slowly becomes apparent. From this standpoint, every estate looks different, from Japan to Cameroon. Suddenly nothing is the same, from the color of the soil, to the shape of the hills, to the surrounding greenery, to the women weaving their way toward the gardens at this early hour.

Dawn breaks over the tea gardens of Asia. *Above:* A plantation in Ceylon, the "Isle of Tea." *Opposite:* Mount Kangchenjunga (28,208 feet), legendary abode of the god Shiva, rises above the Darjeeling district in northeastern India. *Page 20:* Nurturing a new shoot at a garden in Nilgiri, southwestern India. All tea plants belong to the same species—*Camellia sinensis*—although three main varieties exist (China, Assam, and Indochina). Young plants are grown in the shade of a nursery for at least a year before being transplanted into the garden.

DARJEELING

In the northeast Indian region of Darjeeling, between Sikkim, Nepal, and Bhutan, women climb the mountain paths every day at dawn. They make their way toward one of the sixty-one gardens that produce the highly prized "champagne" of black teas on grand estates perched at altitudes of over five thousand feet. The women, strapping Himalaya-dwellers with prominent cheekbones and narrow eyes, advance in single file. Their clothes are poor, but some women wear a silver stud in one nostril. Far behind them, set against the rose-hued sky, loom the eternally mysterious snows of Kangchenjunga, a mountain over twenty-six thousand feet high, said to be the abode of the god Shiva. The women continue to climb above the charming villas and hotels of Darjeeling (where Calcutta's upper middle classes come to escape the noxious monsoon season). They encounter schoolgirls in red dresses and farmers heading for the small village markets. Then, after several winding turns between rock faces on which climbers train, the women finally arrive at the garden.

The garden might be named Castleton, Jungpana, Tukvar, or Badamtam. In Darjeeling, what is called a "garden" is in fact a large plantation sometimes stretching over a thousand acres. But it is still a "garden" because the tea grown here, harvested according to traditional methods, bears its name. Darjeeling's sixty-one gardens produce fifteen thousand tons of tea per year. Its incomparable quality is the result of climate, altitude, and British expertise, plus a disdain for quantity. The wide range of Darjeeling teas is obtained through skillful blending (which varies

A traditional harvest in the Himalayan foothills of Darjeeling, where some of the finest tea in the world—known as the "champagne" of teas—matures at an altitude of 6,500 feet. *Above:* Pluckers working in the rain. Moisture is a key factor in tea cultivation, for the plant requires regular, steady rainfall. *Opposite:* One of the sixty-one Darjeeling gardens at plucking time. The steep mountain slopes, which inhibit mechanization and impose traditional harvesting methods, help to ensure outstanding quality.

according to the altitude of the estate) of the large-leaved plants from Assam with the smaller but robust leaves of Chinese plants. These two main varieties of the single species of tea plant—*Camellia sinensis*—are sometimes crossbred into hybrids. A wild tea plant from China grows six to nine feet high and lives for over one hundred years. An Assam plant can grow to be sixty feet high if unpruned, but does not live beyond fifty years.

Chinese plants, more resistant to cold, are commonly found on plantations in northern Darjeeling, often at altitudes of over six thousand feet. To the south, where plantations are generally located at one thousand feet, Assam plants are more suited to the abundant rainfall.

The diversity of Darjeeling tea is further accentuated by differences in wind and rainfall that depend on the altitude and exposure of the slopes under cultivation. Yet it is seasonal changes that produce the most marked differences. Although tea-lovers cannot always tell a Makaibari from a Puttabong, they can immediately distinguish between a Selimbong tea harvested in spring ("first flush," from late February to mid-April) and the same tea harvested in early summer ("second flush," in May and June), or autumn ("autumnal," in October and November).

The women arrive at the garden just as the sun appears above the snowy peaks. Everywhere in the world, fine tea requires an average of five hours of sun per day. The plantation forms an immense green carpet covering the slopes of the Himalayan foothills. It hugs the dramatic curves, slinking down valleys to riverbeds, climbing to the summit of peaks. It is not unusual for plants to be terraced on 45-degree inclines where

Once picked, tea is immediately dispatched to the factory where it is processed. Transportation time must be kept to a minimum to retain the freshness of the tea, so factories are located on the plantations themselves. Every large garden possesses its own factory. *Above:* The factory at Makaibari, one of Darjeeling's most famous gardens. *Opposite:* A preliminary stage in processing tea in Darjeeling involves sorting freshly plucked leaves by hand to obtain the desired quality.

no machine could ever venture. This mountainous landscape, which requires that the tea be harvested by hand, constitutes a permanent guarantee of quality.

ASSAM

The daily harvesting routine of the women in the upper Assam valley is similar to that of their Darjeeling counterparts, except for a few important details related to differences in climate and geography. The valley is one hundred and twenty miles to the east of Darjeeling, on the border of China, Burma and Bangladesh. At this longitude, the banks of the Brahmaputra (where wild tea plants sixty feet high were discovered in 1823) are among the wettest and least hospitable regions of the world. The valley, hidden between the Himalayas and Mounts Naga and Patkoi, was still overlaid with dense jungle growth when English colonists decided to clear it in the nineteenth century. It remains one of India's least-populated regions, and the mountains are inhabited by tribes whose way of life has not changed for thousands of years.

From April to September, the monsoon unleashes a torrent on the upper Assam valley that swells the river and floods the Ganges delta to the south, in Bangladesh. Every year, these floods take a heavy toll in human life. During the monsoon the temperature rises to 95° Farenheit. It is in this huge, natural greenhouse that nearly a third of Indian tea flourishes, yielding roughly two hundred thousand tons per year, including some of the finest varieties in the world.

Assamese pluckers do not resemble the Darjeeling mountain women. Rather, they are like other women on the Indian subcontinent, with large black eyes and delicate features. Although the image presented by the Tea Board of India shows smiling women in colorful saris and silver bracelets, the realities of climate and vegetation in fact impose particularly difficult working conditions on them.

They harvest eight hours per day in the atmosphere of an overheated greenhouse, and often have to don plastic bags to ward off insect and snake bites. After an overseer has given them the day's instructions on plots to be worked, and indicated assembly and weighing points, the women hoist a large wicker basket on their backs, held in place by a strap around the forehead. Then they advance by rows into one of Assam's two thousand gardens.

It might be Rungagora, Betjan, Silonibari or Keylung. It runs as far as the eye can see, over a stretch of one thousand acres, under large shade trees giving the appearance of a spacious, calm forest. Several hundred women work the garden every day, reaching nearly a thousand pluckers at the height of production between July and September.

In Asia, men are rarely seen harvesting

The upper Assam valley, in northeastern India, is the world's largest tea-producing region. Its two thousand gardens account for almost a third of India's annual harvest of seven hundred thousand tons. Yet it was not until the early twentieth century that the jungle along the banks of the Brahmaputra River, where wild tea plants grew in the torrential monsoon rains, was finally cleared. *Opposite:* The Mituoni plantation, with large shade trees reminiscent of a forest setting, is typical of the huge Assam gardens that sometimes extend over two thousand acres.

tea. It is generally said that the smallness, agility and patience of feminine hands are required for high-yield plucking with no loss in quality. Of course, it is more likely that sociological, economic and even symbolic reasons are behind this tradition, which some people feel contributes to the mysterious charm of tea. Whatever the case, picking tea on a grand estate requires specific skills, particularly dexterity. The women move between the tea plants—small shrubs spaced roughly thirty inches apart, regularly pruned to a height of four feet. With amazing swiftness and accuracy, they gather, with both hands, only the youngest, topmost leaves (which extend above the plane known as the "marker") by snapping the stem with a sharp

movement of the index and middle fingers.

A "fine plucking" of the best teas removes only the terminal bud on the stem—covered with a fine white down—accompanied by the two first leaves below it. Most common teas are produced from a "coarse plucking" that includes the bud and three, four or even five leaves. But in all gardens, the pickers, in an age-old gesture, toss fistfuls of leaves over their shoulders into their baskets. This simple movement acquires the quality of an exploit when one realizes that in Assam, for example, each plucker harvests nearly fifty thousand stems per day. Once the basket is full, the pickers return in procession to an assembly point where the leaves are rapidly inspected and weighed. Pluckers are paid according to the

Plucking is a crucial operation that determines the ultimate quality of the brew. It requires a great deal of dexterity and care. The highest grade of top-quality tea is the product of a "fine plucking" in which only the terminal leaf-bud and first two leaves are picked. *Above:* Picking tea at Blue Mountains, a plantation in southern India. *Opposite, top:* A Bangladeshi woman at work. *Opposite, bottom:* The bud and two leaves harvested during a "fine plucking."

weight and quality of their harvest, generally several rupees (roughly a dollar) per day. Each cup of tea includes its measure of toil.

CEYLON

Milder breezes, lighter, clearer air and a rolling landscape lend the gardens of Ceylon a more pleasant mien. The brightly colored saris scattered among the greenery provide an appropriate touch of beauty. Things exist on a more human scale here, with estates sometimes as small as fifty acres. Most of them are located in the southwestern part of the island. The best gardens are, as always, found at the higher altitudes, from three thousand to eight thousand feet, on the eastern and western slopes of the high plateaus. Depending on the direction in which they face, the gardens are influenced by one of two monsoons; on the eastern slopes, the finest tea is plucked from late June to the end of August, whereas on the western slopes the best harvesting takes place from February 1st to March 15th.

It is now midday at Dimbula or Uva Highlands, Devonia or perhaps Pettiagalla. Tamil women in saris—or rather *lungis*,

Hugh Johnson pointed out that just as the Romans brought vineyards to the countries they conquered, so the English planted tea in India, Ceylon and Africa. *Above:* A garden in Ceylon with its factory and terraced slopes. *Opposite:* A colorful swirl of saris among shade trees in an Indian tea garden.

here—wear a long white cloth on their head to protect their shoulders from the sun. Despite their poverty, they sport silver bracelets, anklets, and gold necklaces. Their graceful and fragile silhouettes, slightly stooped, blend well with the tall tea plants left to grow like trees every thirty feet or so to provide a little shade and mark out the plots. Here and there, men dressed all in white—turban, jacket and long skirt down to their ankles—supervise the plucking. And when the baskets are full, they follow the pluckers to the door of the factory, where the tea is weighed. This tea factory in Ceylon, a long white building occupying the end of a small valley, looks somewhat like an Alpine sanatorium mistakenly set in the tropics. Although the soul of a garden resides in the hands of the pluckers, the factory represents both its heart and brain.

The black teas produced in Ceylon, India and China are the preferred teas in Europe and America. The freshly picked leaves undergo a long process of transformation, for black tea must be fermented. And the fermentation of tea requires as much care and close, scientifically controlled attention as does the fermentation of wine. This industrial

Throughout Asia, picking tea is women's work. It has long been said that only women have the patience and dexterity required for this delicate task. *Above:* Pluckers arrive at an estate in Ceylon's high-altitude Nuwara Eliya district. The long bamboo sticks sometimes used in gardens are placed horizontally at a given height, known as the "marker," indicating the level below which leaves are not to be picked. *Opposite:* Sorting leaves in Ceylon, prior to bagging and weighing them.

art constitutes the modern, technological face of these exotic and apparently unchanging tea gardens, and merits the same detailed description as the colorful swirl of saris. But whereas it is pleasant to linger under a shade tree to watch the plucking, ears lightly humming with the music of wind in leaves or the voices and murmured songs of the pickers, once at the door of the factory it becomes impossible to tarry for long—much less daydream—in the thundering din of machines.

Here, men do most of the work. Barefoot laborers and technicians in British-style shorts bustle among an indescribable clutter of machines, amid dim shade, heat and incessant noise.

Everywhere it is produced, black tea undergoes five successive stages. The leaves are first softened by a withering process that reduces their moisture content by half and enables them to be rolled without breaking. They are spread in thin layers on wide screens stacked eight inches apart to allow a current of warm air to circulate for roughly twenty-four hours. The most modern factories, however, now accomplish the task in tunnels or vats, reducing withering time to six hours.

Withering is followed by rolling (or maceration). The leaves are rolled to break down cell walls and release their essential oils. This was once done in the palm of the hand, but has long since been performed by impressive rolling machines composed of heavy metal disks rotating in opposite directions.

The rolled leaves are then placed on long mats to be sorted according to size and condition—whole or broken. This sorting is still done entirely by hand in some gardens, enabling the leaves to be "graded" into various classes of black tea. In the finest gardens, whole

Each stage in the production of tea takes place within the confines of the estate, from the carefully monitored sprouting of new plants in the nursery to the final packing of leaves ready for consumption. *Preceding double page:* Nursery at the Sangsua garden in Assam. New plants are increasingly being produced from cuttings rather than seedlings. *Above:* A garden in the Nilgiri district in southwestern India. Leaves are aired during the first stage of processing, known as withering, which slightly dries and softens them so that they can then be rolled without breaking. *Opposite:* A basket of freshly picked tea is carried into the factory at Glenloch Tea Estate, central Ceylon.

leaves are classified according to size and the way in which they are rolled, yielding Orange Pekoe (O.P., leaves rolled lengthwise and measuring from eight to fifteen millimeters), Flowery Orange Pekoe (F.O.P., leaves rolled in the same way yet smaller, from five to eight millimeters), Golden Flowery Orange Pekoe (G.F.O.P., an F.O.P. in which certain leaves have a golden tip), or Tippy Golden Flowery Orange Pekoe (T.G.F.O.P., all tips are golden). Leaves that have been broken, deliberately or not, yield high-quality grades of Broken Orange Pekoe (B.O.P.), Golden Broken Orange Pekoe (G.B.O.P.), or Tippy Golden Broken Orange Pekoe (T.G.B.O.P.). Finally, the so-called "crushed" leaves, which are in fact small pieces, are called Dust (less than one millimeter) and Fannings (one and a half millimeters).

Next comes fermentation, the crucial operation that endows black tea with its color and, above all, the subtlety of its flavor. Experts agree that the process remains something of a mystery. No one knows exactly what alchemy produces the flavors, for certain cellular reactions during fermentation have never been fully understood or even identified. We do know that fermentation is produced by exposing leaves to a highly moist atmosphere (at least 90 percent humidity) after having been spread on broad slabs of cement, glass or aluminum. The air temperature must be carefully monitored and controlled (between 72° and 82° F), because a slight rise in temperature will give the tea a burned taste, whereas a slight drop will halt fermentation. When maintained at constant temperature and humidity, the leaf first heats up from the effect of several chemical reactions, then begins to cool off. A tea-maker's skill includes an adept sense of timing—for best results, fermentation should be halted just when the leaf stops heating, which may take from one to three hours.

The leaves are then dried in an enormous machine comprising a dryer and conveyor belt, exposing them to temperatures of at least 175° F for roughly twenty minutes. Drying, the last stage of transformation, also requires well-honed skills. If it is too brief, the tea may become moldy in time; too long, and the tea will lose much of its flavor. All this expertise goes into the black tea that emerges from the great gardens of Asia.

The Tamil pluckers continue to work into the afternoon, repeating the morning's tasks. Meanwhile, several thousand miles away in Africa, on the jungle-covered slopes of Mount Cameroon and the high plateaus of Kenya, dawn is breaking over other gardens that produce several unique varieties of black tea. Here it is men who rise early to pluck the tea planted in the red soil among eucalyptus trees. British planters who left India following independence found favorable climatic conditions in the higher altitudes of Africa. It is said that the chocolate aroma of Broken

Producing black tea requires five successive operations. After the tea is withered, it is macerated (or "rolled")—the leaves are rolled or crushed to release essential oils. Leaves are then sorted according to size and form (whole or broken leaf). The next operation is the fermentation, which transforms green leaves into black tea; the leaves are spread in thin layers and exposed to warm, humid air at a constant temperature for several hours. The final stage entails drying (or "firing") the leaves to halt fermentation. *Opposite:* Tea being fermented at Glenloch Tea Estate, in the mountains of Ceylon.

Three of the stages in the production process—rolling, sorting and firing—were mechanized in the 1880s. *Above:* Once picked, the leaves are set out to wither, then placed in
rolling and drying machines. *Opposite:* Inside a factory near Ootacamund, in southern
India.

Orange Pekoe Fannings (B.O.P.F.) produced on Mount Cameroon became a favorite of the court of England.

CHINA

Although the English taste for black tea taken with sugar and a drop of milk has become the European norm, the vast majority of Asians and North Africans prefer the original green tea that has been consumed in China for over five thousand years. The gardens producing the finest green tea are found on continental China, on Formosa, and in Japan. In China, tea is still made using methods employed from time immemorial. In artisanal cooperative factories, the tea is first steamed for less than a minute in large vats, in order to kill the fermentation enzymes that would otherwise subsequently alter its quality. Next it is kneaded by hand, stacked in small piles, and dried for approximately ten hours, during which time it is regularly turned. The tea is then rolled according to the desired grade, and finally sorted. In Japan and Formosa, these operations are now mechanized. The grades into which green tea is sorted include Gunpowder, used for the finest mint teas in North Africa and the Near East (leaves rolled into tiny balls from one to three millimeters in diameter), Chun-Mee (rolled leaves one centimeter long), Sencha (whole, unrolled leaves, also called "Natural Leaf"), and Matcha (powdered tea used in Japan for the tea ceremony).

No visitor ever set foot in the very best Chinese gardens, which remain shrouded in mystery. Few Chinese even know that these gardens exist, for they are familiar only with the state cooperatives that produce "standard" black and green teas identified by number and skillfully blended to guarantee stable quality whatever the climatic conditions. Certain standard teas are nonetheless high-quality products designed mainly for export, such as Imperial Yunnan from the high plateaus of southern China, or the sweet Imperial Keemun from the mountains of Anhui province. China's secret gardens, however, are kept distinct from these cooperatives, and are called "sacred gardens" by the privileged few. Their exact number—perhaps three or four—is unknown. They are said to be patrolled day and night by police dogs. Why such secrecy? Surely because these gardens produce tiny quantities of superlative green tea that is kept off the market and reserved exclusively for high government officials.

Halfway between the cooperatives and the sacred gardens, China also has gardens producing tea that can be purchased, assuming that one has managed to establish a special relationship with certain authorities. These gardens in the mountainous regions of Sichuan (Szechwan) and Jiangsu yield some of the finest, rarest and of course most expensive

Legend has it that tea was discovered in China five thousand years ago when a tea leaf fell into the bowl of Emperor Shen Nung, seated beneath a wild tea plant. The Chinese plant, which is the hardiest variety, has made China the birthplace of the tea industry. In recent years, the Chinese have discovered numerous giant tea trees growing wild in the country's unexplored southern regions. One of them, over one hundred feet high and with a trunk over three feet in diameter, has been growing in a primitive forest in Yunnan for seventeen hundred years.

In modern-day China, true "gardens" are both rare and secret. Most black and green tea is produced on huge state cooperatives, then marketed in the form of numbered teas of guaranteed standard and quality. Certain outstanding teas are nevertheless given special names. *Above:* Pluckers at work in a cooperative near Hangzhou in Zhejiang province, known for its famous Lung Ching ("Dragon Well"), one of the world's finest green teas.

green teas in the world. Such teas are called Pi Lo Chun ("Spiral of Spring Jade") and Lung Ching ("Dragon's Well"). Yet even these teas seem somewhat ordinary compared to a tea practically worth its weight in gold. This is not a green tea, but white (not steamed, merely dried), a veritable miracle produced in Fujian province known as Yin Zhen ("Silver Needles"). This garden is one of the very few plantations still in existence, almost all of them located on the high China plateaus, that still practice the traditional plucking method formerly reserved for the emperor and a few court dignitaries. Known as "imperial plucking," this method removes only the bud and the first leaf from the bush. Sometimes, as with Yin Zhen, only the bud itself is picked. In the past, nothing was permitted to alter the purity of the plant from the time it was plucked to the moment it reached the emperor's bowl.

Young virgins, gloved and using gold scissors, delicately clipped the stem and placed it in a golden basket, where the leaves were dried prior to being placed in the imperial bowl. No one knows what precautions are taken today to preserve the incredibly subtle aroma of "silver needles," which reminds the most sophisticated palates of the fragrance of orchids. All that is known is that the tea is plucked only once a year, during two days selected according to minute botanical observations. Should unanticipated wind or rain arrive during those two days, the annual harvest is purely and simply canceled.

FORMOSA

China offers no glimpse of its sacred gardens, nor does it like to show its large estates to foreigners. Moreover, these plantations often

In the People's Republic of China, mists and fog often compensate for insufficient rain-fall, at the same time cloaking the gardens in secrecy. Here tea is produced according to ancient, time-tested methods, and workers perform all tasks by hand, just like their ancestors. *Above:* A plantation on the island of Hainan, to the south of the mainland. *Opposite:* A plucker in Szechwan, one of the six main tea-producing regions in China.

remain veiled in mists or, as in Fujian province, hidden behind screens of smoke from the spruce pine that yields its fragrance to Lapsang Souchong before wafting from the factory chimney. The smoke only clears sixty miles to the east, in the sky over the strait of Formosa, off the coast of Taiwan. Here, in full view and to the great delight of demanding tea-lovers from Hong Kong and Singapore, the great Chinese teas of yore are being reborn. Rich merchants, bankers and shipping magnates now buy extravagantly expensive green tea in Formosa, tea harvested and produced in small family gardens with artisanal methods, exactly as it was done in imperial China. Approximately one hundred families thus produce Oolong, the island's great specialty, a so-called "semifermented" tea because it undergoes only an initial stage of fermentation. Its taste and color are halfway between green tea and black tea.

This one-day, whirlwind tour of the world's finest tea gardens reaches northern Formosa in the afternoon. Here, in a small mountain chain, a superior semifermented tea known as Ti Kuan Yin ("The Goddess") is grown. It is reputed to eliminate all impurities from the body. Formosa benefits from an ideal climate for growing tea—very humid, with temperatures never rising above 82° F in summer yet never dropping below 55° F in winter. The harvest lasts eight months, from April to November. Mr. Chang, a small independent

tea-grower, displays medals won during the annual Ti Kuan Yin contest on the rustic walls of his office. Through the window, pluckers can be seen working in the mist. Like all the best Formosa teas, Mr. Chang's Ti Kuan Yin is not available through normal export channels involving brokers, telexes or commodity exchanges where tea is auctioned to importers the world over. Any foreign buyer who wants Mr. Chang's tea must go straight to the grower, at least the first time. If the buyer is lucky, the wind will disperse the mist for a moment or two, and the lofty gardens of Ti Kuan Yin will offer a vantage point from which to contemplate the entire north end of the island, from Taipei to the sea twelve miles away.

JAPAN

This tour of the world's tea gardens in fact provides a good opportunity to survey some impressive landscapes, to surrender to the fascination of endless vistas, enigmatic mists, gargantuan mountains. For thousands of years, the landscape in which tea is grown—so propitious to contemplation and meditation—has brought mankind closer to the heavens, if not the gods. It is probably no coincidence that it was a Buddhist monk named Saichô, a member of the Tendai sect, who first brought tea plants to Japan from China early in the ninth century. Three or four hundred years later, Zen monks would

Tea cultivation was introduced into Japan in the ninth century by a Buddhist monk. To this day, tea remains an integral part of Japanese spiritual life. Thus the magnificent gardens dotting the islands seem specifically designed to encourage meditation, like Zen rock gardens. *Opposite:* Motionless waves of tea in a garden in the Shizuoka district to the west of Tokyo, where most of Japan's green tea is grown.

drink a large bowl of Matcha, a powdered green tea rich in vitamins, in order to perform long hours of meditation without flagging. In Japan, tea began and then spread as an accompaniment to spiritual exercise. So it is hardly surprising that the nation's tea gardens are works of art

as sublime as Zen rock gardens, even if they do not necessarily have the same symbolic import.

Japanese tea gardens are unlike any others. It is sometimes hard to believe that tea is being grown on them. From a distance, they look like vast stretches of some vivid green liquid that veils the hills, frozen into motionless waves. This effect is due to the way the bushes are planted and pruned; they are not spaced apart, as elsewhere, but are placed sided by side to form lengthy, tight strips thirty yards long, whose uniform and slightly curved surface forms an enormous plucking table. All these strips are identical in size, planted in parallel rows roughly a yard apart, perpendicular to the slope. Except perhaps in Java or Bali, with their terraced rice fields, no other growers have managed to sculpt the land so beautifully. But everyone knows that, in Japan, the functional is inevitably beautiful.

Japan produces only green tea, known as O-Cha. It is grown in the Mount Fuji area, on the island of Kyushu, and in Shizuoka, the main growing region known for its infinite variety of the most common tea, Sencha. In winter, hot-air fans protect the tea plants from the threat of frost.

The afternoon wanes delightfully in the Uji countryside, near Kyoto, where natural springs spill down the finely carved emerald hills. In the garden, women in long red aprons glide slowly between the motionless waves. They pluck what some people consider the finest green tea on the planet—Gyokuro, "Precious Dew." Nowhere else (except, perhaps, in China's sacred gardens) is tea cultivated with such care. Three weeks before the harvest, as soon as the first buds appear, the entire plantation is covered with mats of bamboo, reed or dark canvas to filter out 90 percent of the light. The tiny leaves that grow in the semi-darkness thus have a higher chlorophyll content (hence the emerald green color) and a lower tannin content (rendering the tea less bitter). Gyokuro is the mellowest of green teas. Like the rare teas of China, it is harvested only once each year, in late April or early May, according to the imperial method that removes only the bud and, if quality allows, the first leaf. Once reduced to powder, the

In characteristic Japanese fashion, sophisticated technology coexists with centuries-old tradition. Gardens are sometimes heated in winter by electric radiators, and harvesting machines move through rows of tea plants without diminishing the quality of the finished product. *Above:* Mechanical harvesting at a Shizuoka garden. *Opposite:* Traditional wicker baskets filled with tea leaves. Green (that is to say, unfermented) tea, the only kind produced in Japan, is made by steaming the leaves, then drying and rolling them. To obtain the Matcha tea used in the tea ceremony, the leaves are pulverized into a powder.

precious tea from this garden becomes Matcha Uji, the most subtle of Matcha teas, used in the traditional Japanese tea ceremony.

TEAS THE WORLD OVER

India, Ceylon, China, Formosa, Japan, Cameroon and Kenya are not the only countries with fine tea gardens. Some of the other twenty-three tea-growing countries also offer high-quality specialty teas. Indonesia, for instance, boasts Java Taloon, although this variety may not long withstand the drive for profitability now sweeping the islands, spurring growers to produce ordinary teas for teabag consumption. Sikkim, a small Indian protectorate in the Himalayas, produces a Temi rivaling the best Darjeelings. Nepal, with its Everest plantations, also produces fine tea.

In other countries, where intensive and fully mechanized production methods are used, there are no "gardens." In parts of the former Soviet Union, once the world's fourth largest producer, machines straddle hedges of tea bushes planted as far as the eye can see in the plains of Georgia, the Caucasus, and Azerbaijan. Such tea is satisfactory for everyday use, but not for the sophisticated palates

of certain privileged officials who pay a fortune for the finest Darjeelings on the Colombo exchange in Ceylon. (Colombo employs a reverse auction system—a maximum price is announced, and the first bidder to match or to come closest to that price carries the lot. In the two other major international exchanges, London and Calcutta, dozens of brokers buy and sell the finest teas according to a conventional auction system.) Turkey and Iran in the Near East, Brazil and Argentina in South America, and Tanzania, Malawi and Uganda in Africa also produce average-quality teas usually destined for teabags.

The tour returns to Darjeeling as evening falls. In the nursery of a garden such as Singtom or Selimbong, technicians monitor the growth of young *Camellia sinensis* plants. These cuttings are raised for two or three years under a shelter of woven branches. When they are nearly two feet high, they are planted in the garden.

Not far away, in a well-lit room at the factory where the machines have just fallen silent, a hundred white porcelain cups—filled with infused tea and topped with a cover—are lined up on a large table. Each is placed between an empty bowl and a small vessel filled with dry

The large international tea exchange in Colombo, Ceylon during a power failure.
Unfazed, the tea brokers continue to trade by candlelight.

tea. A man pours the contents of the cups into the bowls, through the sieved cover that stops the leaves. This cover, full of steeped leaves, is then turned upward. Once the operation has been completed, the garden's official taster examines the dry leaves, the steeped leaves, and the color of the liquid in the bowl. He sniffs the tea, tastes it, then spits it out in a large basin that he pushes before him as he goes along. He makes notes in a heavy ledger. Every day during the harvest, prior to packing, the produce of each plot in the garden is subjected to this quality-control tasting.

Prior to reaching retail shops all across the world, the finest teas will be tasted in this way at least four more times. Once by the broker (or his taster) who then sends samples to importers. And then three more times by the importing expert, who then places orders with the broker. Another tasting takes place after the tea has been bought at auction (in Colombo or Calcutta), just prior to shipping, to verify that the bulk product corresponds to the original sample. A final tasting occurs when the tea has reached its port of destination, to make sure that shipping has not affected quality. Naturally, these multiple tastings are not performed on "standard" China teas (due to predictable quality), nor on the ordinary teas used in most blends.

The day-long tour draws to a close. It has now been several hours since the pluckers left Darjeeling's gardens. Tea harvested the day before has just been packed in chests whose corners are sealed shut with aluminum plaques. As the sun sets, enormous pink and black clouds appear over the mountains. The wind murmurs through the leaves, barely disturbing the silence. The soil in the garden, depleted by the long day, awaits the rain.

This chapter was written with the expert assistance of Mariage Frères tea dealers, Paris.

The day draws to a close in the tea gardens. *Above:* The tasting room of a factory in southern India's Nilgiri district, where teas similar to those from Ceylon are grown. A tea maker prepares a subtle blend of leaves that were plucked the preceding day, and which have just emerged from the dryer. *Opposite:* This blend being packed in chests is a green gunpowder tea, the basis of the finest mint teas consumed in North Africa.

· TEA ·

BARONS

Nadine Beauthéac

66 Toward the end of the seventeenth century, the English on leaving Canton placed on board their ship chests covered with brass-wire panes, filled with good soil in which they had sown excellent tea seeds; during the crossing, care was taken to water them regularly with fresh water and to avoid exposing them too much to the air and salt water dew carried by breezes across the waves. It was thanks to these meticulous precautions that the first samples of this shrub were introduced into England."

This botanical experiment, described by J. G. Houssaye in his *Monographie du thé* (Monograph on Tea), was only partly successful. Once planted in experimental gardens, the bushes indeed grew to maturity. But under English skies, the plants developed leaves whose quality was unfortunately inadequate for producing tea. A century and a half later, however, the English would begin to compete with China by becoming tea-growers in their own right, and would soon become the undisputed masters of the international tea trade.

Europeans had discovered tea earlier. It was around 1606 that the Dutch East India Company imported the first shipments of tea from China after striking a good bargain—it acquired three measures of tea for each measure of sage.

In Amsterdam, London and Paris, tea was drunk as early as 1635. But it was still an expensive luxury known only to Europe's high society. Moreover, like other herbal "decoctions," tea was essentially appreciated for its therapeutic properties, even though there was no universal agreement over this. Right into the early eighteenth century, the benefits of tea were a subject of debate at the Sorbonne. France's Cardinal Mazarin drank tea to prevent gout, whereas Samuel Pepys noted in his diary that his wife found it a remedy for her colds and bronchitis. "However," continued Houssaye in his monograph, "the way to prepare tea was scarcely known in England except in several houses in the capital. . . . The widow of the unfortunate duke of Monmouth sent a pound of tea to one of her relatives in Scotland without indicating how it was to be prepared, and the cook boiled the plant, tossed out the water and served the leaves like a dish of spinach!"

The Dutch lost no time in realizing that buying and selling this new merchandise could be as profitable as the spice trade. Beginning in the 1630s, therefore, they adopted the habit of loading several large pottery jars of tea

Above: After a long, drawn-out crossing, tea seeds that had been smuggled out of the Chinese Empire's forbidden regions arrived at European nurseries in poor condition, at least until the botanist N. B. Ward invented an efficient container for them. Henceforth plant species coveted by the West, notably the tea plant, could make the crossing safely. *Opposite, top:* The Dutch trading post and warehouses on the Japanese island of Deshima. This artificial island in the port of Nagasaki was created in 1634 to house the Dutch and Portuguese, since foreigners were not allowed on Japanese soil. In 1641, a Dutch firm set up a trading post that operated there until 1858. *Opposite, bottom:* Philippe-Sylvestre Dufour's *Traités nouveaux et curieux du café, du thé et du chocolat,* 1685. *Page 56:* A Lewis Carroll photograph of a little girl in Chinese Mandarin costume, circa 1880.

Chinois auec son pot de Thé.

Thé de la Chine sur sa tige.

Traité Nouueau & Curieux du Thé
Composé Par Philippe Syluestre Dufour

223

TRAITÉ DU THÉ.

CHAPITRE I.

De la nature du Thé, de son nom, des lieux d'où il vient & de l'ancienneté de son usage.

E Titre que j'ay donné à ce Livre, & le raport qu'il y a entre le Café & le Thé, m'invite aprés avoir

K 4

onto each vessel returning from China. By 1669, the East India Company, the British equivalent of the Dutch firm, also began regularly importing tea, and immediately began envisaging measures against potential competitors who might want to enter the business.

On 3 August 1700, the *Amphitrite*, the first French ship to leave for China, brought back tea from Canton along with Chinese silk, lacquers and porcelain. Within one hundred years, a taste for tea had been acquired throughout a Europe mad for exotica—tea was now appreciated for its rarity rather than for its medicinal properties. The infatuation with tea was not an isolated phenomenon. In fact, in a mixture of snobbery and genuine interest, Europe adopted everything that came from faraway shores—lacquered screens, cloisonné enamels, silk, muslins, calico, china, and so on. And just as a pagoda became an indispensable part of every respectable landscape garden, so chocolate, tea and coffee were served in all the best homes of Europe.

Right from the first public sale—which

By the mid-eighteenth century, the East India Company possessed a fleet of over one hundred ships, and boasted superb offices in the center of the City of London. In Canton, meanwhile, the company's representatives had to deal with vexing restrictions and uncertainty. Company officials had long resisted the idea of sending a special diplomatic mission, which they feared would further irritate the Chinese. Yet in 1792, when Lord Macartney's expedition left Portsmouth, the East India Company's three-masted, twelve-hundred-ton *Indostan* set sail alongside the Royal Navy's *Lion. Above:* An East India Company vessel being outfitted at a Thames shipyard, circa 1660.

took place in 1657 in London, in a coffee house owned by Thomas Garraway—the English took a shine to tea. The government quickly sought to cash in on the craze by levying a tax on imports in 1660. The tea trade would be subject to this tax until the 1780s.

Since demand was great (tea having slowly replaced beer as the beverage of poor families), methods for dodging the tax became widespread. Servants in upper-class homes, for instance, would dry used leaves and resell them. Small industries began to prosper as tea was cut with various ingre-dients like beech, hawthorn and logwood. Smuggling China tea into Europe spread all the more rapidly insofar as London traders encouraged it; the French and Flemish coasts were used as ports of call for smugglers who then unloaded their cargoes at night in Cornwall or Wales. The British exchequer and the East India Company were aware of the extent of their losses. Only a large cut in the tax rate could make legal imports compet-itive with contraband goods. This finally occurred in 1784 with the promulgation of the Commutation Act.

Prior to sailing, Macartney interviewed Company agents formerly stationed in Canton. They painted a grim picture of the European ghetto: "The 'factories'—huddled one against the other, with the flag of each country flying in front—were rat-infested holes. The conditions in which His Gracious Majesty's subjects lived were worthy neither of the epoch nor of British subjects. Westerners were denied all contact with the Chinese, who were forbidden to teach their language to the Barbarians under pain of death." Alain Peyrefitte, *L'Empire immobile. Above:* The Canton "factories," painted by William Daniel, circa 1785.

China, for its part, was unable to meet rising European demand. It began placing poor-quality tea on the market. The main concern of the East India Company (which came under direct government control following the Commutation Act) was to obtain the best trade conditions with China, given that country's monopoly as the world's only producer.

But China remained a land of mystery, since travel into the interior was strictly forbidden. Canton, the tea port, was the assembly point for chests that arrived from distant producing regions to the north, but no European had ever been permitted to enter the city itself. Commercial transactions were conducted exclusively by the Co-Hong, a consortium of authorized merchants who paid a tax to the emperor for the right to retain a monopoly business.

In 1793, George III decided to "cultivate friendship with China" and dispatched the costliest diplomatic mission ever sent by a Western nation to Peking. The mission was headed by Lord Macartney. The English had hoped to be allowed to trade freely with China, but negotiations were a failure—the Middle Empire barely tolerated the presence of Western "barbarians" and clung faithfully to its principle of complete self-sufficiency. But the Chinese underestimated English cunning. England had already gone to war to break the Dutch monopoly on spices, and it now decided to wrest control of the tea trade from a China that insisted on being paid in hard cash.

Thanks to their colonies in India, the English managed to produce goods valued in China. First with cotton from Bengal and later, in 1773, with opium, the East India

Company found a satisfactory product with which to finance its purchases of tea. The drug traffic was illegal, however, so the Company discreetly employed private companies to act as go-betweens.

A taste for opium grew swiftly throughout all layers of Chinese society. But it was the educated class, senior civil servants and the sons of wealthy families who were the largest regular consumers, despite imperial edicts. When the Chinese authorities attempted to block this trade, England started the opium war that finally won it numerous trade concessions, including the opening of several Chinese ports, the use of the island of Hong Kong as a trading base, and the end of the Co-Hong monopoly. The British, however, were already considering another way to supply themselves with tea. They wanted to cut China out of the business altogether.

The botanist Sir Joseph Banks, who accompanied Macartney's mission in the hope of bringing tea plants back to the botanical garden in Calcutta, had declared in 1788 that the Indian climate would be favorable to the cultivation of tea. This idea was backed by David Scott, an agent of the Governor General in Assam, who wanted to develop the region he supervised. The English then seriously considered acclimating tea bushes to their Indian territories. But little was known about how to grow and process tea, for the Chinese jealously kept these things secret.

Lord Bentinck, appointed governor of India in 1828, made it possible to acquire

British sailors who arrived in Canton sought presents to take back home. Highly prized souvenirs included genre scenes and portraits painted in the Western manner by Chinese artists. These images began appearing in the eighteenth century and became known as "China Trade Paintings." They represent an artistic version of "East meets West," for a typically Chinese sense of encyclopedic detail was fused with a Western rendering of perspective and shading. *Above:* A China Trade Painting of the Canton customs house, circa 1800. *Opposite:* Business cards distributed by British tea dealers in the eighteenth century. *Preceding double page:* An eighteenth-century China Trade Painting of Chinese officials receiving officers of the East India Company.

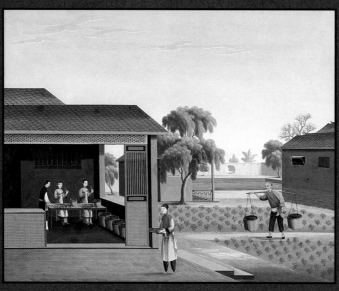

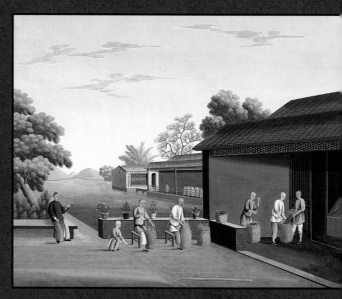

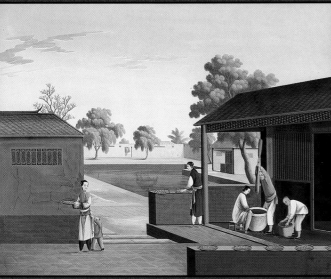

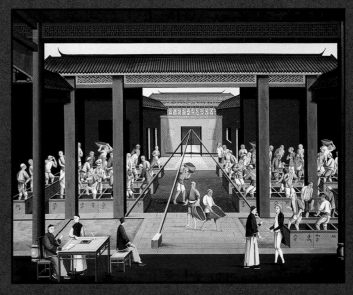

the needed information by setting up the Tea Committee in 1834. The committee included seven agents of the East India Company (which had lost its monopoly on the tea trade the previous year), three Calcutta tea dealers, and two eminent Indians. This association sowed the seeds for the first tea plantations in the British empire, estates that would soon be in a position to rival those of China.

AN ENGLISHMAN NAMED FORTUNE

Two centuries after tea was first brought to Europe, it had become relatively easy for foreigners passing through China to obtain tea plants. The Tea Committee sent several botanists to China, instructing them to choose good plants, gather information about cultivation methods, and recruit Chinese growers to emigrate to India to start plantations. In 1834, J. C. Gordon collected over eighty thousand seeds and dispatched them to nurseries in Calcutta. The English had observed that the numerous varieties of tea all came from the same plant, *Camellia sinensis*. The different teas therefore depended on climate and especially on processing techniques. But the secret of how to actually produce tea remained totally unknown. It was an Englishman named Robert Fortune who finally solved the mystery of Chinese tea.

Fortune had already spent three years in China before he returned there in 1848 on behalf of the Tea Committee. His goal was to

The earliest European photographers in China produced "exotic" images from their studios in Hong Kong, but they were soon supplanted by photographers more interested in documenting everyday life. John Thomson's photo essay, photographed between 1868 and 1872, reveals a China probably quite similar to the one that Robert Fortune discovered. *Above and opposite:* Sedan chair and Chinese coolies, photographed by John Thomson, 1868. *Preceding double page:* A series of China Trade Paintings by the Cantonese watercolor artist Tingqua (1840-1870), depicting various stages in the cultivation and production of tea: preparing the field, sowing, watering, harvesting, sorting, withering, fermenting black tea, firing, grading the leaves, packing, local distribution, and crating for export.

Above: Sorting leaves in a Canton tea factory. Photograph by John Thomson, 1869.
Opposite: Throughout China, taking a break involved not only tea but also tobacco, which had been brought to China by the earliest Spanish and Portuguese explorers. The resulting fanatical consumption of this product probably paved the way for opium. This penchant for tea and tobacco was exported to the Chinese Empire's vassal states, as illustrated by this Annamite man in Hanoi smoking a pipe while his tea steeps, circa 1870.

explore the regions where the finest teas were produced, areas still off-limits to foreigners. Fortune first headed roughly one hundred and twenty miles north of Shanghai, where the most famous green tea grew. He was accompanied by two Chinese companions who suggested the ruse that would enable him to accomplish his mission—they showed him how to disguise himself as a Chinese merchant. To avoid prying eyes, the three men left Shanghai on a junk at night, and they were extremely discreet when arriving at towns, tea houses and inns.

Fortune was carried in a sedan-chair, from which he could observe the hillside tea plantations, most of which were small family farms. He tirelessly studied soils, manual plucking techniques, and processing methods. In the evening, he prepared crates to be shipped back to botanical gardens in Calcutta and Kew, and recorded the day's observations in his journal, which he planned to publish on his return.

Thanks to Fortune, the fabulous world of tea finally became comprehensible to Europeans. One of the mysteries he solved concerned the "blue tea" so prized in Europe and America—in fact, it was nothing other than green tea colored with gypsum powder. The Chinese themselves never drank this "barbarous" concoction, producing it merely to satisfy foreign demand.

Fortune made another important discovery. During a visit to the famous Buddhist temple in Kooshan, an old priest led him to a spring in a natural setting of great beauty. The monks diverted the cool, clear water to a little reservoir, next to which a teapot was constantly heated. Fortune was offered a bowl of tea—the best he had ever tasted. He immediately realized, of course, that the flavor of tea is intimately linked to the quality of the water in which it is brewed.

On return to Shanghai, Fortune had accomplished only part of his mission. He still had to visit the regions

One of the earliest instances of what is today called "industrial design" entailed decorating the chests used to export China tea. By the end of the seventeenth century, these wooden chests were adorned with sheets of paper illustrated by factory artists. The patterns were adapted to Western tastes, for Europeans were drawn to "chinoiseries" that bore little relation to native pictorial tradition. Initially painted by hand, this packaging paper was later printed, and often bore the exporter's trademark. *Above:* Eighteenth-century tea chests. *Opposite:* Manufacturing tea chests in China, circa 1880. Chests were lined with metal foil.

that produced black tea. He took to the road again, donning his usual disguise and accompanied by a Chinese friend who knew the area thoroughly. During the day, he visited tea factories, where he pretended to be a mandarin from Mongolia. In the evening, he stayed in monasteries.

The regions that produced black tea astonished him even more than had those producing green tea, for he learned that tea was transported from these plantations to Canton entirely on the backs of men. The trip required a month of steep and difficult climbing on mountain paths that were practically washed away during the long rainy season.

Certain coolies carried just one chest, which was never allowed to touch the ground. An ingenious system involving a bamboo triangle resting on the shoulders enabled them to set their load against a wall when they wanted to halt. This type of transportation was reserved for the finest teas, whereas more ordinary varieties were carried in more traditional fashion, that is to say two chests attached to both ends of a bamboo pole balanced on the shoulder. At each halt, however, these chests would inevitably touch the ground, and the Canton merchants realized that this altered the quality of the tea.

On returning again to Shanghai, Fortune placed his samples in "Ward cases" that allowed the seeds to germinate on board the ship during the long return trip. Then he descended the Yangtze to Hong Kong, where he sailed for Calcutta. He was accompanied by eighty-five Chinese specialists headed for the small plantations then being cleared in northwestern India. Meanwhile, an amazing discovery was made in Assam.

THE ASSAM JUNGLE

In 1823, the East India Company received a report from Major Robert Bruce, a Scot who had learned during conversations with local tribal chiefs that a wild tea plant grew in Assam. The altitude and weather conditions in this region, located on India's eastern border with China, were in fact similar to those in the Chinese provinces of Szechwan and Yunnan, where the finest tea was produced.

In 1834, the Tea Committee founded by Lord Bentinck confirmed the existence of wild tea plants in Assam. This discovery fueled dreams of growing tea in India on a major scale, creating gardens that might one

In China, tea was usually shipped along waterways. But when rivers were not navigable or mountains had to be crossed, an efficient but costly system of porters was used. Westerners were invariably impressed by the porters' prowess: "The Chinese have more strength than might be expected from a people nourished solely on rice and water." Hans-Christian Hüttner, *Voyage en Chine, 1792-1794. Above:* A porter carrying a chest of tea, 1902. *Opposite:* Carrying bricks of tea to Tibet, 1908. Each man covered approximately six miles per day, laden with three hundred pounds of tea.

day rival those in China. Seeds from Chinese tea plants brought back by Gordon and Fortune were distributed to colonists in various Indian provinces, making them the British Empire's first planters. At the same time, the Tea Committee sent Charles Alexander Bruce, Robert's brother, to Assam to conduct an experiment using tea plants of local origin. A former lieutenant in the Royal Navy, C. A. Bruce was one of the first Europeans to enter Assam's thick forests. This region, one of the most rain-drenched in the world, was not easily accessible. For four years, aided by two Chinese experts brought back by Gordon, Bruce located tea plants, then cleared and burned away the surrounding jungle to create a plantation. It quickly became apparent that Bruce's techniques produced excellent results, whereas the conventional efforts using Chinese plants were stagnating.

In 1838, the *Calcutta* sailed from Assam for London with twelve chests of tea in her hold. The January 1839 auction of this first crop sparked enthusiasm among the brokers on Mincing Lane (the tea and colonial commodities market). This constituted the turning point long sought by the English—the British Empire had produced its own tea. It then seemed feasible to send colonists to Assam to extend the plantation system. The British government launched a recruitment campaign, dangling the dream of easy riches before a crush of volunteers. Successful candidates had to sign a contract with the Assam Company (founded in 1839)

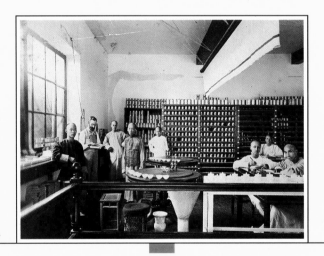

British tea tasters acquired their art by adopting the time-honored methods of Chinese tasters. *Above:* In Shanghai, a European dealer samples tea, surrounded by Chinese colleagues. Tea cups are placed on the rotating table, accompanied by hourglasses that determine steeping time. A ceramic spittoon can be seen on the floor—professional tasters never swallow the teas being assessed.

"An 1868 investigatory commission . . . acknowledged the unhygienic conditions of the Brahmaputra and Soorma valleys where the plantations were located. At low altitudes, the ground was often flooded; heavy monsoon rains and high temperatures produced swampy breeding grounds for malaria-carrying mosquitoes. . . . There was also a food supply problem, since the few existing rice paddies constituted a drop of water in an ocean of undeveloped jungle. . . . It was a forest in which even an elephant had a hard time advancing." Paul Butel, *Histoire du thé. Above:* Elephants clearing a plantation in Assam, circa 1880.

until the firm lost its monopoly in 1850. Yet budding planters were not told until they arrived in Calcutta after a six-month voyage that they would have to sail on a steamer up the Brahmaputra for another twenty to thirty days before reaching Nazira, where the Assam Company had set up a trading post in a still-unexplored region. Nor were they told that they would complete their journey on elephant, through dense jungle, carrying several months' supply of rice—a grueling trip from which many would not return.

Once they arrived at their destination, the colonists were housed in bamboo huts furnished with a few crates. Their first task was to clear the jungle and select tea plants. An initial harvest took place the following year, after which the nurseries grew and plantations developed. As soon as possible, planters would build a bungalow offering, at last, a less rudimentary lifestyle. But they had to learn to abide solitude, for they planted far from one another and often had to travel by ship or elephant to supervise the work of extending their own plantations. A candle or kerosene lamp was their only company at night, whether at camp or in the bungalow. Wild beasts roamed after nightfall, and planters had to be good shots. In addition, the unhealthy climate placed them at the mercy of diseases such as malaria, cholera, yellow fever, and dysentery.

Over the decades, planters slowly improved their living conditions; the arrival of their wives played a major role in establishing a social life. By the 1880s, bungalows managed by memsahibs who received guests in European style no longer bore any resemblance to the huts of the early days. Imitating habits back home, families would dress up on Sunday to go to the club, where planters would engage in games of polo and cricket. Hunting became a favorite pastime. Meanwhile, the Assam Company had built roads, organized a regular ship service as far as Nazira, and built warehouses along the river to facilitate the delivery of supplies.

In 1881, a railway line was finally opened. At that point, five hundred and eighty planters were living in Assam, one hundred and thirty in Bengal (notably Darjeeling, which would produce the finest Indian tea), and forty in northwestern India.

The jungle that had discouraged numerous planters and taken the lives of many others was equally harsh on local employees who worked on the tea plantations. Once estates grew large, finding labor became a problem. Workers were recruited in Bengal, along the banks of the river that flowed down from Assam. In Calcutta, go-betweens made a fortune by recruiting hundreds of coolies with promises of good wages and easy work. A large part of this labor force would die during the long and difficult voyage. Those who reached the plantations worked without respite and without health

"Ah, sir, volumes could be written on the tea industry in Assam. Just imagine—on one side you have the English, driven by the desire for profit, sometimes mixed with a sincere wish to civilize the Assam jungle, and impatient and violent because they are unsure about their future on the commodities exchange. On the other side you have the wretched Hindus from the south, driven from their homes by poverty and hunger." Ferdinand Goetel, *Voyage aux Indes*, 1937. *Opposite:* A late nineteenth-century photograph of Indian women on the plantation waiting for their harvest to be weighed.

care; their ranks were decimated by disease.

Some planters attempted to regulate recruitment and working conditions. But this often meant that coolies signed away their rights—a coolie who broke his contract could be sent to prison, and at the end of the contract he had to pay his own way home. Fully one-third of a plantation's employees died on site, for they were underfed, housed on swampy, mosquito-infested ground, and worked in monsoon rains. Women and children were subject to the same work rules as men. Absenteeism and attempted escape were punished by flogging. The Assam planters were often compared to American slave owners—Assam was said to produce "bitter tea."

The situation deteriorated during the recession that occurred in the 1860s. Labor problems were complicated by the new planters' lack of experience, for they were often retired officers or former shopkeepers. They had invested in several acres of jungle land in the hope of striking it rich, yet knew nothing about cultivating tea. By stressing quantity over quality, planters encouraged the chaotic extension of tea crops and the ill-considered importation of an inefficient workforce.

It was not until the 1870s that Assam tea became competitive once again, and regulations protecting workers were not truly enforced until 1930.

"Tea planters have become the masters of Darjeeling. In the future they will be able to overcome all obstacles, bridge the abyss, traverse forests and put Darjeeling in touch with the rest of the world. For the moment, however, Darjeeling is still a bizarre camp of nomads from the north, perched atop a wild mountain." Ferdinand Goetel, *Voyage aux Indes. Above:* Darjeeling, photographed by Phillip Ellis in the late nineteenth century. *Opposite:* Another Ellis photograph, this time of leaves being rolled by hand.

Meanwhile, several plants from Assam had reached Ceylon. This little island in the Indian Ocean would become a major producer of tea thanks to another wave of pioneers spurred by famine in Scotland.

THE LOOLECONDERA ESTATE

Nothing predisposed the island of Ceylon, a British crown colony since 1802, to such a fate, for tea plants did not figure among the local flora. Yet from the early nineteenth century, several enthusiasts used their estates as experimental plots. In 1839, Dr. Wallich, head of the botanical garden in Calcutta, sent several Assam tea plant seeds to the Peradeniya estates near Kandy. This initial consignment was followed by two hundred and fifty plants, some of which went to Nuwara Eliya, a health resort to the south of Kandy, situated at an altitude of 6,500 feet. The Nuwara Eliya experiment produced entirely satisfactory results. Seeds of Chinese tea plants, brought to Ceylon by travelers such as Maurice de Worms, were also planted in the Peradeniya nurseries. But this time the results were disappointing, and Chinese plants were gradually abandoned in favor of the Assam variety that is now grown on every estate in Ceylon.

Tea cultivation nevertheless remained a minor activity for twenty years. The island's prosperity in fact derived from coffee, whose quality rivaled that of Brazil. This situation changed dramatically in 1869 with the outbreak of a parasite fungus, *Hemileia vastatrix*, that systematically destroyed coffee

The bungalows built by tea planters and other British civil servants in India inaugurated an architectural style that typified nineteenth-century Anglo-Indian buildings. The roof extended beyond the walls to create a shaded veranda, supported, if necessary, by pillars. Later such verandas, usually embellished with an arcade or peristyle, would become a characteristic feature of villas and palaces in Colombo and Calcutta. *Opposite:* Planter's bungalow and tea factory on an estate in Ceylon, circa 1890. *Above:* Planting seedlings in Ceylon, circa 1890.

plants. Tea then appeared as a godsend, and the entire local economy shifted to the new crop in a matter of several years. This rapid substitution owed a great deal to the fruitful initiative of a man named James Taylor.

Back in 1851, near Mincing Lane, Taylor had signed on for three years as an assistant supervisor on a coffee plantation in Ceylon. This sixteen-year-old Scot, son of a modest wheelwright, would never see his native land again. But throughout his life he sent letters to his father back home, providing a unique description of the daily life of a planter in that epoch. Five years after he took up his post, his employers, Harrison and Leake, impressed by the quality of his work, put Taylor in charge of the Loolecondera estate and instructed him to experiment with tea plants. The Peradeniya nursery supplied him with his first seeds around 1860.

Taylor then set up the first tea "factory" on the island. It was in fact a rather rudimentary setup. Historian D. M. Forrest quotes a description provided by Taylor's neighbor, planter E. G. Harding: "The factory was in the bungalow. The leaf was rolled on tables on the veranda by hand, i.e. from wrists to elbow, while the firing was done in chulas or clay stoves over charcoal fires, with wire trays to hold the leaf. The result was a delicious tea which we bought up locally at Rs. 1.50 per lb." The factory soon became famous throughout the island. In 1872, Taylor invented a machine for rolling leaves, and one year later sent twenty-three pounds of tea to Mincing Lane. Taylor trained a number of assistants, and from that point on Ceylon tea arrived regularly in London and Melbourne. Its success led to the opening of an auction market in Colombo in 1883, and to the founding of a Colombo tea dealers' association in 1894.

Taylor continued to test new methods and techniques at the Loolecondera estate (which he would never own) until the end of his life. He was well-liked by both European planters and native workers, yet remained somewhat solitary. He never left the estate, except for a single short vacation in 1874—spent at Darjeeling, needless to say, in order to study the new tea plantations. His talent and determination were officially recognized when Sir William Gregory, governor of Ceylon, paid Taylor a visit in 1890 to congratulate him on the quality of his tea. The Ceylon Tea Growers' Association, founded in 1886, gave him a silver tea service engraved with an inscription citing his pioneering work.

But the rise of the tea industry nurtured by James Taylor was also the cause of his downfall. Rapid growth was accompanied by a concentration of capital in the hands of large corporations based in Britain, and a wave of property consolidation forced out smaller planters. Taylor, like other planters, was dismissed. Terribly disappointed, he decided to remain on his estate despite an order to quit;

"At six o'clock, the day is done; all the workers gather at the factory, where their harvest is checked and weighed. The first operation performed on the leaves is the withering. . . . Then the leaves are churned in a cylinder for roughly twenty minutes, before being spread on plates of glass where they ferment for two hours. Then, in a current of hot air, they are sorted on a screen of metal wire. . . . The women sort small and large leaves into two separate baskets. After this, the tea is packed in metal-lined crates. These chests are sent to Colombo, from whence they are shipped the world over." Fia Öhman, *Impressions de Ceylan*, 1925. *Opposite:* Packing tea into chests, Ceylon, circa 1890.

not long afterward, in 1892, he died suddenly of dysentery at the age of fifty-seven, on his beloved soil at Loolecondera.

The 1884 and 1886 International Expositions held in London introduced the English and foreigners to teas produced in the British Empire. But it was at the 1893 World's Fair in Chicago that Ceylon tea made a tremendous hit—no less than one million packets were sold. Finally, at the Paris Exposition of 1900, visitors to the Ceylon Pavilion discovered replica tea factories and the "five o-clock tea" that became so fashionable. As a contemporary chronicler put it, "The charming colonial house with bright shutters, the deliciousness of the beverage, the beauty of the Singhalese people—living statues of bronze wrapped in shimmering white loin-

cloths—everything contributes to the success of this delightful stand at Trocadero. . . ."

The planters' association supported this propaganda campaign by organizing various publicity events. In 1891, Kaiser Wilhelm II, Czar Alexander III, Grand-Duke Nicolas, the queen of Italy and Emperor Franz-Josef all received sixty coffers of tea accompanied by an illustrated album on Ceylon.

The promotional policy was so effective that by the end of the nineteenth century, the word "tea" was no longer associated with China, but with Ceylon. The island's prosperity sparked covetousness on the part of British companies and London brokers, who wanted to acquire their own plantations and cut out the middlemen. This marked a turning point in the saga of tea—pioneers gave way to

After the First World War, Great Britain was no longer in the forefront of the international tea trade. Added to this were a sharp rise in unemployment and social unrest. To stimulate the economy and promote solidarity, the government launched a campaign to encourage British subjects to buy Empire products—wool from New Zealand, oranges from South Africa and, of course, tea from India and Ceylon (which were able to supply all of the British Empire's tea-drinking needs). *Above and opposite, top:* Empire Marketing Board posters. *Opposite, bottom:* An advertisement reminding consumers of Lipton's success at the 1893 World's Fair.

merchants, whose name or label would soon become more important than the country in which the tea was grown.

THOMAS TWINING'S GOLDEN LYON

The fantastic expansion of the tea trade in England during the 1880s enabled several British merchants to impose their brand the world over, creating veritable financial empires. These empires were sometimes the stuff of childhood dreams, built by combining cleverness with a certain sense of humor and outrageousness.

Such was the case of Julius Drewe. He opened The Willow Pattern Tea Store in Liverpool in 1878, the name of his store evoking the Chinese-style pattern on a type of plate then greatly appreciated by those enamored of exotica. The willow therefore became the emblem of an amazing success story. Drewe was born in 1856, and started his career in a firm owned by his uncle, a tea importer. The young man was made a buyer, traveling a great deal and acquiring a fascination for Asia. He nevertheless decided to settle down and open his own store in Liverpool, followed by a chain of Home and Colonial

Stores in the 1880s. Soon six hundred of these shops dotted the country. The firm's success had a strong impact on the tastes and habits of British tea drinkers. By frequenting Drewe's establishments, which promoted the importation of Indian tea, consumers acquired a taste for flavors that differed from those of China teas.

Having acquired a considerable fortune by the age of thirty-three, Drewe was admitted into English high society and was notably befriended by the prince of Wales. To compensate for the suddenness of his social rise, he delegated the management of his business to his partners and began to look into his family genealogy. Discovering that he had aristocratic forebears, he decided to spend his fortune on building a castle to commemorate his ancestors and his noble origins. He chose the most talented architect of the day, Sir Edwin Lutyens, to design the castle (Lutyens became famous for having constructed the palace of the viceroy of India in New Delhi, among other buildings). Work began in 1911, but was not completed until 1931. Castel Drogo still stands in the wild Devon landscape, but its owner did not have time to enjoy it, having died the very year

British importers had to convince consumers that their brand was better than the competition. Twinings' advertising played on the company's image as "suppliers to the aristocracy." Some firms sold sugar—at a loss—with their tea, while others offered maps of London or illustrated almanacs. Promotional gifts became common at the end of the nineteenth century. On buying a given quantity of tea, customers would receive table linen, teapots, infant high-chairs or even money. *Above:* An eighteenth-century Twinings business card. *Opposite:* Twinings promotional cards, 1900 and 1920.

his castle was completed.

While Drewe was still opening his first store, the Twinings had already been well established for five generations. Tea merchants from father to son, they were all brilliant traders and constituted a dynasty whose fate was closely linked to the destiny of tea in Europe.

Thomas, the founder of the line, was born in 1675. He was the son of Daniel Twining, a weaver by trade. Since the paternal firm offered few prospects, the entire family moved to London in 1684. In 1706, Thomas started his own business by opening a café, known as Tom's Coffee House. This new establishment on the Strand had plenty of competition—London's business district included over two hundred and fifty coffee houses at the time. But "Tom's" was the first to systematically encourage the sampling of tea by the cup, which probably explained his swift success. Writers, poets, doctors and jurists got into the habit of meeting there to discuss art or politics, and Twining soon opened a second room to the public. In 1717, he bought the building next door in order to open a retail store. Not only did it sell tea leaves and coffee beans by weight, but women—who were not welcome

in coffee houses—were allowed to consume beverages on the premises.

The Golden Lyon, as Twining's establishment was known, did not merely supply private customers. Little by little, the firm specialized in wholesale marketing, supplying all retail tea outlets in London and the provinces. These included pharmacists, innkeepers and even goldsmiths, for grocers had not yet begun to stock the product. Thomas soon increased the volume of his imports (which came from China, via the East India Company). When Thomas's son Daniel joined the firm in 1734, Twining became a family concern whose successive representatives have upheld its reputation to the present day. It took just two generations for the marketing network set up by Thomas to expand significantly by moving beyond Britain into continental Europe, America and the West Indies. This success was not simply due to luck. Twining heirs were initiated into the business at an early age and moved into positions of responsibility by their twentieth birthday. They then stuck with the firm, sometimes until their death, and often played a leading role in the tea trade.

Tea was at the height of its popularity in 1880, and tea dealers prospered mightily. The Twinings, henceforth at the head of an internationally known company, put some of their profits into philanthropical causes. Thomas Twining founded a science and hygiene museum, and authored books designed to edify the working classes. His sister, Elizabeth, founded Saint John's Hospital in London. *Above:* The Twinings shop in Paris, photographed circa 1900. It still exists today on Boulevard Haussmann. *Left:* A 1900 advertisement. *Opposite:* The accounts register for the Twinings firm in London.

Thus Richard I, Thomas Twining's grandson, became chairman of the association of Dealers in Tea. Richard II (1778-1857) presided over the arrival of fast clipper ships that brought their Asian cargoes home in ninety days instead of six months. He exploited his father's heritage so well that he became official supplier to Her Majesty Queen Victoria in 1837, as well as supplier to the prince of Wales in 1863. To this day, the famous firm still boasts these official distinctions. As to Richard III (1807-1906), he realized that a top-quality product could easily resist the onslaught of marketing innovations. For a new approach was revolutionizing the way tea was marketed—it was henceforth sold in packets rather than in bulk. It was Horniman, a small merchant from the Isle of Wight, who perfected this idea as a means to prevent adulteration of the final product. Horniman was soon selling five million packets per year. But Richard III remained unmoved by this argument. He preferred to wager on prestige and tradition. Nor was he wrong, for his clientele included palaces and grand hotels as well as connoisseurs who bought in bulk to make up their own blends.

Twining nevertheless began selling tea in packets in 1930, as well as teabags. And it was in 1939 that the Twinings moved into Ceylon, finally bypassing the middlemen they had employed for generations. Despite these changes, however, the venerable firm remained remarkably faithful to the spirit of its founder. Even to this day, a Twining still heads the business, and the sign of the Golden Lyon can still be seen over the original store.

Clippers built from 1850 onward at the Aberdeen, Glasgow and Liverpool shipyards competed in the famous annual "Tea Race" to determine who would be the first to unload the new harvest of China tea after a globe-spanning, 16,000-mile regatta. *Above:* The *Cutty Sark* never won the race, but achieved fame by reaching London after having lost its rudder in the middle of the Indian Ocean. The *Cutty Sark* is the only clipper surviving from that glorious period, and can be visited by the public at Greenwich, on the Thames. *Opposite:* Tea dealers' shops in Newcastle, circa 1900, and a 1900 ad for Horniman's Tea (*inset*).

Compared to the saga of the Twining family, the story of Thomas Lipton is that of a solitary man who relied only on himself and his own business acumen. He created such a marketing empire that within a few decades his name became inextricably linked with Ceylon tea. Some people even muttered that Ceylon was not a British colony but a Lipton colony.

As a child in Glasgow, where he was born in 1850, Lipton worked at the small family grocery and displayed an aptitude for business. At age fifteen, he left for America, where he survived by doing odd jobs on plantations in the south. Four years later, however, he was employed in the food section of a New York department store. That is where he acquired most of his keys to success.

Studying American marketing methods, he thoroughly absorbed the principles of a new sales strategy—advertising. He immediately applied these principles on his return to Scotland in 1869 by organizing a publicity stunt around his own arrival. He left the ship's cabin only at nightfall, attaching the ostentatious gifts he had bought for his mother to the roof of a carriage that he then raced through the streets of Glasgow under the windows of his fellow citizens, making sure that the entire city was aware of his return. But the young man's father refused to disrupt his little trade by adopting American methods. The twenty-five-year-old Thomas, endowed with five hundred dollars in savings, thus decided to start his own business. Five years later, in 1880, he headed a chain of twenty general stores. By 1890, he

Three weeks after first setting foot in Ceylon, Thomas Lipton had become the island's main property owner. But his entry into the world of tea was not effortless, as he himself noted in his memoirs. "I would not like you to imagine that in these early Ceylon transactions . . . everything 'came off' for me as easily as if I had been shelling peas. Far from it. A lot of hard thinking had to be done and much more hard work. . . . I had to apply myself diligently to a completely new set of facts and circumstances." *Above:* Pluckers in the Lipton garden at Dambatenne, Ceylon, circa 1900.

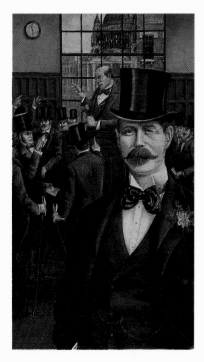

owned three hundred. He had become rich and popular by age forty. His innate sense of publicity and theatrical flair won him a large following, drawn by the street parades and amusing attractions that accompanied the opening of each new store.

In 1890, Lipton sailed on a purported trip to Australia. His true destination, however, was Ceylon. Ever since the 1880s "tea boom," Mincing Lane brokers had attempted to convince him to stock tea on his shelves alongside the hams and cheeses. They felt that Lipton's enormous network of outlets would boost sales further. Lipton decided to look into the affair himself.

When he arrived at the Grand Oriental Hotel in Colombo, Lipton was not yet aware that his life had reached a turning point. He did, however, immediately realize that he had arrived at just the right moment. Ever since the outbreak of the disease that ruined coffee plantations, land in Ceylon was being sold at ridiculously low prices. Lipton went to visit the estates at Dambatene where he purchased—for half the amount he had expected to invest—four tea plantations. He

Despite the backing of his personal friend, Edward VII, the highly successful Lipton was stymied in his attempts to join the most famous yacht club in the world, the Royal Yacht Squadron in Cowes. The official reason was that Sir Thomas lacked sailing experience, the unofficial reason being that he had begun his career by "selling hams." Lipton was only admitted thirty years later. On learning the news, he is reported to have sardonically inquired as to the whereabouts of the club to which he had just been admitted. *Above:* Portraits of Lipton visiting his Ceylon gardens, on the veranda of his bungalow, and in a London auction room.

would soon advance from a millionaire's status to that of a billionaire. He reorganized the plantations and instituted innovations still new to Ceylon, such as rolling machines, dryers and cable-car systems to transport the harvest from the steep slopes to the factory.

At that time, a pound of tea cost three shillings in London, which Lipton thought too expensive for an average middle-class family. He calculated that, thanks to the elimination of middlemen, he could continue to make a profit even while bringing the retail price down to one shilling and seven pence. He decided to market his tea in packets, offering a reliable product of standard weight and quality. Finally, he coined his famous slogan: "Direct from the tea garden to the tea pot." The inauguration of the initial sale of tea at Lipton stores was marked

by a huge parade—two hundred of Glasgow's unemployed, specially recruited for the occasion, dressed up in Singhalese costumes and marched behind the cavalcade.

Furthermore, the product itself was improved, for the firm's tasters were instructed to ensure that the tea suited the water of each region, which might be more or less hard. The blends on sale therefore differed from one town to the next. Lipton then coined a new slogan: "The perfect tea to suit the water of your own town."

When Lipton left Glasgow, following the death of his parents, to set up his company headquarters in London, his name became a nationally known brand. In 1894, only four years after his trip to Ceylon, his London staff numbered five hundred, and his plantations, factories, stores and warehouses employed ten thousand

When a journalist asked Lipton for the secret of his success, the magnate replied that it lay in having no secret at all. Advertising was the key: one should never let an opportunity go by without exploiting it. Lipton pulled off his biggest publicity stunt in 1924 without so much as lifting a finger—a town in Canada was named after him. *Above:* Tins of tea. *Below:* Delivery van. *Opposite:* Sacks of tea on a Ceylon plantation.

people. Business was so good that the ambitious Lipton was spurred to expand his empire even further.

So he set out to conquer the American market. He first obtained samples of tea sold in stores in New York and Chicago, and had them analyzed in his Glasgow laboratories; it turned out to be green China tea of ordinary quality that shopkeepers displayed in open chests, taking no particular care over proper storage. Lipton therefore established his American network by insisting on the correct conservation of tea. The quality of his tea merited several prizes at the 1893 Chicago World's Fair.

Having reached the height of success and fame—he would be ennobled in 1902—Thomas Lipton finally devoted himself to sailing, his childhood passion. He became one of the most famous challengers for the America's Cup and launched several superb racing yachts, all named *Shamrock* after the very first boat he had carved as a child with a knife from his father's store.

The British public avidly followed the acts and exploits of this character, who despite his unsuccessful cup challenges, remained "the tea gentleman." He spent winters in New York and summers in Ceylon (where he was nicknamed "Tea Tom"), and continually surprised his contemporaries. Some described him as a sentimental old man who wandered alone through London's slums, giving chocolate to poor children. Another anecdote sheds a different light on the personality of this incorrigible businessman. When the ship on which he was traveling ran aground in the Red Sea, the crew lightened the vessel by tossing the cargo overboard. Lipton grabbed a brush and can of red paint to daub the chests drifting toward shore with the following message: "Drink Lipton's Tea. . . . "

Above: Before leaving London to compete for the America's Cup in 1929, Thomas Lipton posed on the train platform at Waterloo station with a woman selling Lipton tea. *Opposite:* Tea arrives at the London dockyard of Butler's Wharf, where working conditions were not unlike those of the factories in India and Ceylon. From left to right: receiving the shipment, inspecting the chests, bulking the tea to measure the shipment, repacking in chests, weighing, buyers examining samples, dispatching the chests, children labeling tins for retail distribution. These warehouses have now been transformed into a lively residential neighborhood.

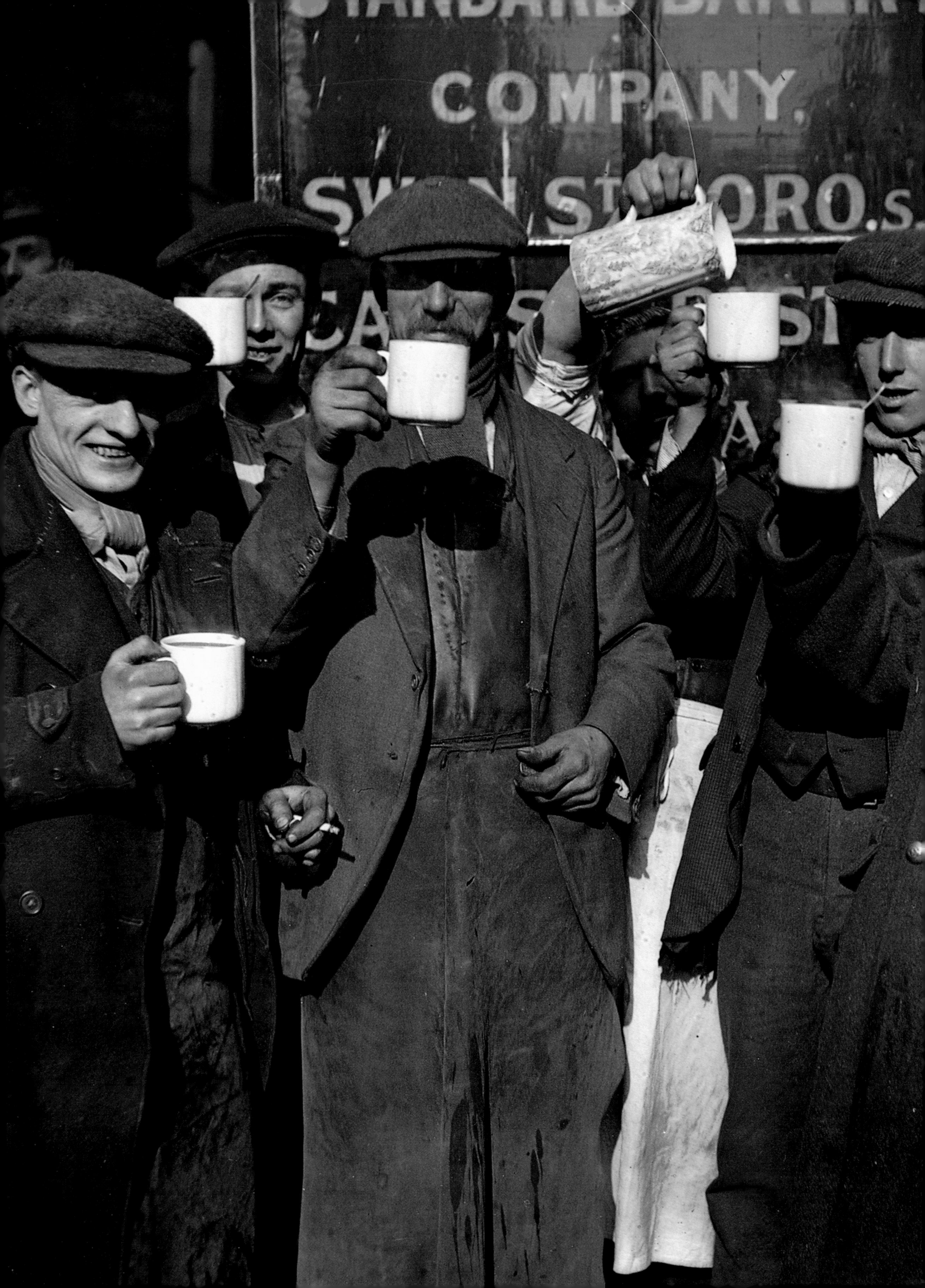
COMPANY,

· TIME ·

FOR TEA

Gilles Brochard

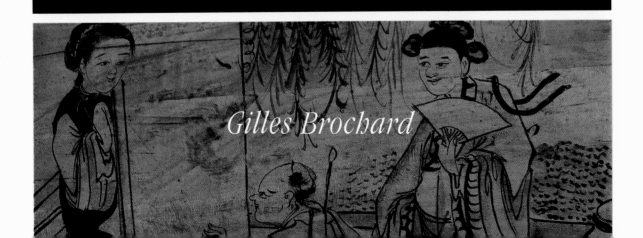

More tea is drunk, worldwide, than any other beverage—except water. From China to England, from India to America, and from Japan to Morocco, tea has acquired a vast multitude of followers, leaving its mark on every civilization. Each day, over one and a half *billion* cups of tea are consumed on the planet. This success is due to the fact that tea has been able to adapt itself to the cultures it has encountered. For, unlike modern soft drinks that sweep across the planet with the help of colossal advertising campaigns, tea has never been perceived as a threat to a way of life, has never been synonymous with uniformity. It is not generally a ready-made beverage consumed straight from a can or bottle. To the contrary, tea requires a sometimes lengthy rite of preparation, stimulating an inventiveness that is conducive to the free expression of individual tastes. Many different attitudes and cultures are thus encountered along the route that leads from a steaming bowl of *cha* with yak butter to a tall glass of iced tea with lemon, from ceremonial Matcha to *thé au lait*.

CHINA, BIRTHPLACE OF TEA

Ever since its lucky "discovery" by Emperor Chen Nung in 2737 B.C. (a leaf from a wild tea plant reportedly fell into his bowl of hot water), the first three thousand years in the history of tea were a purely and intensely

Above: A French advertisement for "mandarin-flavored China tea" (probably a scented blend), circa 1900. *Opposite:* A photo taken from *The English at Home*, a photo essay created in the 1930s by the famous photographer Bill Brandt. *Page 100:* Tea break at a London factory, circa 1930. During the Depression, employers resisted the idea of a tea break, but British labor unions made it a bargaining issue alongside wage demands.

Chinese affair. In *The Chinese Art of Tea*, John Blofeld noted that every layer of Chinese society played a part in this history, including "emperors and peasants, Taoist recluses, Buddhist monks, wandering physicians, mandarins (the scholar-officials of old China), lovely ladies, craftsmen, potters, poets, singers, painters, architects, landscape gardeners, nomadic tribesmen who bartered horses for bricks of tea, and statesmen who used tea to buy off would-be invaders. . . . "

Even though China, unlike Japan, never transformed the drinking of tea into a sacred ceremony, it nevertheless initiated the time-honored ritual of offering a bowl of tea to a guest as a sign of welcome. This tradition was reportedly begun by a disciple of Lao Tse named Kuanyin who one day offered the "old philosopher" a cup of the golden elixir. Thus by 500 B.C., tea had become what it remains today in many countries, especially in Asia—a mark of friendship and hospitality. Once associated with Taoist philosophy and therefore intimately linked to the rise of Zen Buddhism, tea was also thought to provide the energy required for meditation.

But it was not until the flamboyant T'ang dynasty (A.D. 618-907) that tea, long drunk and appreciated for its medicinal properties, became an object both of veneration and flourishing trade. Highly prized at court, it acquired followers throughout the empire, winning converts in Tibet and among nomad-ic peoples living beyond China's northern and western borders, such as the Mongols, Turks and Tatars. The shrewd imperial government profited from this infatuation by taxing the tea trade. During the same period, the poet Lu Yu composed a paean to tea in the form of the *Chaking*, the first history of tea. Generations of tea dealers subsequently worshiped Lu Yu as a sort of patron saint. He inspired numerous disciples, including Lu T'ung, nicknamed the "tea maniac." Lu T'ung was a Taoist poet born at the end of the eighth century who lived aloof from the world, in Hunan, where he became one of the first "tea masters." Venerated by his contemporaries, Lu T'ung devoted his life to poetry and the preparation of tea, occupations summed up in a now famous line of poetry: "I am in no way interested in immortality, but only in the taste of tea."

Under the T'ang dynasty, tea was glorified by poets and codified by tea masters, becoming the quintessential beverage of refined souls. The art of pottery also made great advances during this period, evolving toward more sophisticated forms and techniques. Teapots and bowls in engraved gold and silver even came into use until tea masters categorically forbade the use of metallic utensils. Tea was usually drunk in large wooden bowls. Water was boiled in terracotta vessels, and the tea itself came in the form of leaves, powder or cakes. Connoisseurs

"Everywhere in Chinese towns one encounters large shops where people go solely to drink tea. These shops house square wooden tables around which are placed benches and chairs. In the back is the laboratory . . . stocked with countertops carrying enormous kettles and huge teapots." William Milne, *La Vie réelle en Chine*, 1850. *Below:* A nineteenth-century teapot in red clay, from Yixing. *Opposite, top:* The Woo Sing Ding shop in Shanghai, circa 1900, that reportedly inspired the so-called "willow-tree pattern" used on English porcelain. *Opposite, bottom:* Tea house in Nanking, circa 1930.

preferred it in this latter form, for it could be broken into larger or smaller pieces that were crushed into powder prior to preparation.

The art of tea reached its height from the tenth century onward, under the Song dynasty, also famous for its pottery. In order to obtain the finest tea, everyone sought to perfect each stage of preparation. The quality of the water, the quality of the tea plant, and especially the type of utensil (like the little grinder used to crush tea leaves or the cleft bamboo stick used to stir the water) took on considerable importance in the eyes of tea-lovers. The wooden bowls used during the T'ang era were replaced by larger, shallower vessels called *chien*. Soon tea contests became fashionable, notably among highly placed government officials. Zealots would jealously keep their brewing techniques secret, going so far as to travel alone to seek

water from a preferred mountain spring.

Emperor Hui Tsun (1100-1126) encouraged this search for perfection, even complaining of the "waste of so much good tea through improper handling." As painter, poet and playboy who delighted in the company of courtesans, the emperor was sometimes criticized for placing pleasure over duty. But everyone recognized his expertise at preparing tea, and the emperor's treatise on tea, *Ta Kuan Ch'a Lun*, became the connoisseurs' bible. The book praised the virtues of a drink that freed the mind from stress, both physical and mental, thus making it possible to forget the world for an instant and attain total serenity. The emperor's own serenity required a particularly pure form of tea. The "imperial plucking" method obeyed strict rules and was used only for the emperor's tea: the leaves were picked

The jasmine tea usually served in Chinese restaurants in the West is falsely exotic, since the Chinese themselves do not drink tea during meals. In fact, they do not drink anything during meals, except on special occasions when alcoholic toasts are offered. Tea is nevertheless widely consumed between meals, all day long. It may be drunk in the street (where traditional hawkers still sell it) or at the office (thanks to enamel thermos bottles). *Above and opposite:* Street hawkers in Canton today, and in a village of the past. *Preceding double page:* A nineteenth-century painting illustrates two ways of serving tea—a teapot and ordinary cups can be seen on the table in the back, whereas the servant carries covered cups in which tea is brewed directly.

by young virgins wearing gloves and using gold scissors; they cut only the bud and the youngest leaf, which were left on a golden platter to dry before being poured directly into the emperor's bowl.

Not all Chinese could aspire to such a degree of purity. In Hangzhou, the Song capital in southern China, high-ranked civil servants gathered in tea houses known for their luxury, their warmth, their magnificent floral decorations and calligraphed scrolls, and their excellent "plum flower" alcohol accompanied by delicacies—not to mention the music lessons also given there. Less wealthy tea-lovers generally called on the services of street hawkers. But they could also go to working-class tea houses that Marco Polo felt were of dubious propriety, since somewhat bawdy ladies enlivened the atmosphere with song.

Following a long period of conflict sparked by the Mongol invasion and subsequent rebellion against the heavy taxation imposed by the invaders (tea not being exempt from the general hike in tribute demanded), China slowly returned to stability with the Ming dynasty, founded in 1368 at Nanking. The production of tea increased and techniques evolved—old-fashioned bottles for boiling tea were replaced by kettles and, since it was no longer conceivable to drink tea "like some thirsty ox," rustic wooden bowls were replaced by tiny cups of fine porcelain. Tea leaves were no longer boiled and stirred, but merely steeped, which meant that the teapot became the most important utensil in preparing the beverage.

This typically Chinese method of steeping tea soon found followers on another continent. Tea and China porcelain arrived in Europe at the beginning of the seventeenth century on Dutch East India Company ships. At the same time, the use of tea leaves spread across Japan and Korea, countries that had consumed tea in powdered form until that point. In Korea, where by the eighth century the art of tea was as refined as in China, a little ginseng was often added to the brew.

As the centuries passed, tea became a staple in China, along with salt, rice and vinegar. Up until the 1950s, people from all walks of life drank tea during the day, whether at home, in tea houses, or at work. In private homes, the tradition of offering tea to guests—even unexpected ones—was upheld. Tea was kept hot in large teapots nestled in quilted baskets. It was not unusual for a storekeeper to offer customers a bowl of tea, and tea was often made available to hotel guests in their rooms. In cities from Peking to Canton, tea houses opened at dawn to welcome those who, an hour after sunrise—the moment when vital energy is at its purest—would be out strolling with their caged pet birds. These early customers would be followed by tradesmen, apprentices, and

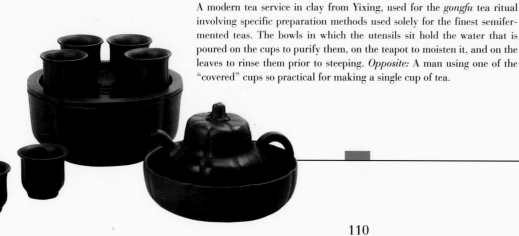

A modern tea service in clay from Yixing, used for the *gongfu* tea ritual involving specific preparation methods used solely for the finest semifermented teas. The bowls in which the utensils sit hold the water that is poured on the cups to purify them, on the teapot to moisten it, and on the leaves to rinse them prior to steeping. *Opposite:* A man using one of the "covered" cups so practical for making a single cup of tea.

workers. In tea-producing regions, villagers liked to gather in the finest tea houses in the world, those in the midst of the plantations, near a pure mountain spring.

John Blofeld, who spent thirty years in China, described a student picnic that he attended in the hills north of Chongqing just after the Second World War. The fire was fanned with a dry banana leaf that replaced the "broken fan" usually employed for such rustic operations. The tea was prepared on a charcoal stove. Each guest drank four bowls of green tea. Then an unusual game began, in which Blofeld participated. The game involved composing a poem on a given subject—the spring water. Blofeld mumbled a few words on the theme, in English, and his poem was submitted to general criticism. Fortunately, his honor was not impugned and the "true spirit of tea" prevailed.

Although tea is still drunk at home in China, most of the tea houses disappeared during the "cultural revolution," along with traditional tea celebrations and the drinking of tea in public. The art of making tea and relaxing over a cup was designated as an "unproductive leisure activity," and therefore practically forbidden. China has nevertheless pursued a policy of massive exportation and carefully cultivates its "sacred gardens," small plantations where the imperial plucking method is secretly employed to supply top government officials with the finest green and white teas in the world.

In recent years, however, some tea houses have begun to re-open, such as the Red Lantern in Chengdu, where storytellers bring Chinese feudal traditions back to life.

For the Muslim population in Kashi, the largest urban agglomeration in western China, tea-drinking traditions bear little resemblance to Chinese customs but are more closely related to those of the caravan routes beyond the border. *Above:* In Kashi, after men leave the Id Kah mosque following the Friday prayer, women solemnly offer them bread and tea. *Opposite:* Famous teas rooms in Shanghai (Xu Xing Ting, *top*, Mandarin Garden, *center*) and in Macao (Loc Koc, *bottom*).

The Way of Tea

A disciple of Sen Rikyû, the great tea master, once asked, "Can you tell me exactly what, above all, must be understood and kept in mind during a tea ceremony?" The master answered: "Make a delicious bowl of tea; arrange the charcoal to heat the water; arrange the flowers the way they are in the fields; in summer, suggest coolness, in winter, warmth; anticipate everything; be ready for rain; show the greatest possible consideration toward your guests."

These few words express it all. In the sixteenth century, Rikyû codified the current tea ceremony, known as *cha-no-yu* (literally, "hot-water tea"). His advice, appreciated and faithfully followed by subsequent generations, was capped by a final comment. "Tea is nothing other than this: heat the water, prepare the tea and drink it with propriety. That is all you need to know."

The "Way of Tea" incarnates all the poetic beauty of Japanese spiritual philosophy. The ceremony is performed in a private tea house called the *sukiya*, which might be translated as the "Abode of Vacancy." As pointed out by Kakuzo Okakura in his 1906 *Book of Tea*, each celebrant knows that the ceremony is "more than an idealization of the form of drinking—it is a religion of the art of life." Celebrants should therefore religiously follow the strict rites established in

the sixteenth century, a ritual inspired by Chinese Buddhist monks. The tea used is Matcha, or "froth of liquid jade," a powdered green tea that is not steeped but whipped in the bowl with a small bamboo whisk called a *chasen.*

Yasunari Kawabata wrote that "a tea ceremony is a communion of feeling, when good friends come together at the right moment, under the best conditions." The ceremony is by nature simple, yet codified down to the smallest detail. Prior to entering the "Abode of Fancy" or "Abode of Vacancy," guests must cross a garden by a path of paving stones, the *roji* ("earth damp with dew"). They walk silently, leaving worldly sounds behind. Trees, moss and bird-song help instill a mood of concentration. Establishing harmony with nature is an indispensable prelude to the ceremony, and it extends to the waiting room where several flowers are placed in a bamboo vase. Sometimes, prior to leaving the garden, the host (who has silently greeted his friends) invites his guests to perform the purification ritual of rinsing their mouths and washing their hands in a small stone basin.

The central room where the guests sit is decorated by a hanging scroll, parchment or painting, selected according to the day, the season, or theme of the gathering. The host enters via a sliding door, and serves a light, quintessentially Japanese meal, *kaiseki*, to

"As dusk gave way to the first stars, the women arrived, bowing delightfully. . . . Spicy pickled fruit was passed around on cleverly shaped trays. There then appeared transparent porcelain cups, the size of half an egg, from which the ladies drank a few drops of sugarless tea poured from doll-like kettles." Pierre Loti, *Madame Chrysanthème. Opposite:* Two engravings by Toshikata, dated 1905, from a series of prints on the tea ceremony—arranging accessories (*top*) and bidding farewell to the guests (*bottom*).

each of the guests seated cross-legged on mats. Each dish, served in simple yet refined crockery, comes from either the sea or the mountains. Food is to be savored in three ways, according to Soshitsu Sen—"with the eyes, the tongue, and the heart." Guests use freshly cut chopsticks of green bamboo, making the contact of food and mouth all the more pleasant. At the end of the meal, the host offers everyone a syrup-drenched cake or a delicacy made of white bean curd (*namagushi*). Guests may then get some fresh air in the garden, prior to sitting down once again to drink the strong tea.

The host carefully handles the required instruments—the teapot containing Matcha, the tea spoon, the *chasen*. Water is heated in a kettle placed on a charcoal stove sunk into the middle of the floor. Tradition demands that guests share the same bowl, each awaiting his or her turn. The host—who does not partake—patiently repeats the preparation, never forgetting to greet the person who extends his hands for the bowl. Guests must hold the bowl in both hands, with the porcelain pattern turned toward the host. The tea, with its fine avocado hue and slightly starchy taste, will be drunk in this way three times. Every object is then

conscientiously washed and put away in the alcove. Then the host returns and offers a cake to each guest, followed by weaker tea served in a different bowl. The tea ceremony concludes in silent contemplation of the fire and the surroundings. The host accompanies his friends to the threshold, then carefully puts away the utensils, removes the flowers and sees to the cleanliness and order of the tea house.

"In the eyes of an uninitiated observer," notes Soshitsu Sen, "nothing extraordinary happens. The host and his guest nevertheless expect this experience to constitute a microcosm of life itself." Learning to perform the tea ceremony requires long training, and Japanese children take lessons after school hours, just like music or dancing lessons. Instructors must serve long years of apprenticeship before becoming qualified masters. Women, whether or not they come from a family with a strong tea tradition, have been allowed to perform the ceremony since the beginning of the twentieth century if they receive the approval of a grand master.

Although the tea ceremony is still practiced today, it obviously encounters the complications that go with modern Japanese life. For it can only be performed inside

Felice Beato's photographs, taken in the 1860s, document Japanese traditions just prior to the industrialization and Westernization of the country. The prints were colored by hand, using a Japanese method then unknown in Europe, adding an unusual dimension to these scenes of everyday life in which tea seems to be a constant feature. *Above:* Guests at an inn. *Opposite:* Woman at her toilet, and a strolling street hawker.

The Urasenke Foundation in Kyoto is the most famous of the three Japanese schools of tea. *Above:* Inside the foundation, a gateway and *roji* (path of stones and pine needles) lead to the "tea room." *Opposite:* The tea master's house, and one of the rooms in which the "Way of Tea" is taught.

a private tea house made of specific materials, conforming to certain proportions, and set in a garden.

The mistress of an ordinary house may nevertheless perform the ceremony if a room is set aside for that purpose. She will invite her guests, in writing, three or four weeks in advance of the occasion, perhaps in honor of the arrival of a friend in town, or the blossoming of the cherry trees, or simply to admire the moon.

As to public tea houses, they had their moment of glory in Japan in the seventeenth century. They were true pleasure houses, where people bawled out songs and played music. They often had rooms where guests could spend the night.

Recent modernization—or rather, Americanization—has led to a drop in the consumption of tea in Japan, in favor of other beverages. Japanese green tea is drunk early in the morning to get a good start on the day, or before a meal to help digestion, thereby losing its sophistication and becoming an everyday drink. In the past ten years, the Japanese have tended to replace this leafy green tea first by semifermented tea and then, after a period of transition, by black tea that is sometimes sold in nylon teabags. The latest craze seems to be for scented blends and flavored tea (such as apple tea), often imported from France and therefore known locally as "French tea." True tea-lovers hope that the Japanese, and in particular Japanese youth, will gradually rediscover the "Way of Tea." For tea remains deeply etched in contemporary Japanese culture—it is the only country in the world to elect a

The great tea master Rikyû was suspected of having betrayed his lord, and was therefore obliged to commit suicide. He organized a final tea ceremony, at the end of which he broke his bowl with these words: "May this cup, soiled by the lips of misfortune, never serve another man." *Above:* Utensils employed in the tea ceremony, including the kettle and the ladle used to scoop water. *Opposite:* A craftsman makes the little whisk used to whip the mixture of water and powdered tea (Matcha). *Following double page:* The tea ceremony in Japan. Japanese men have recently begun to attend classes on the tea ceremony as a way to relax after a long day's work.

"Miss Tea" each year to promote the year's harvest. Artists and filmmakers also often pay homage to the role of tea, as seen, for instance, in Yasujiro Ozu's film *The Bitter Flavor of Green Tea over Rice.*

TEA FROM TIBET AND INDIA

High on Himalayan pastures, shepherds occupying the mountain huts in springtime may well offer a passing traveler salted tea with goat's milk. This is common practice among Tibetans, who often replace the goat's milk with yak butter. Their green, salty tea is generally accompanied by the famous *tsamba,* a flat cake of ground parched barley or corn, mixed with buckwheat and kneaded into balls.

In the mid-nineteenth century, Father E. R. Huc's *Souvenirs d'un voyage dans la Tartarie, le Tibet et la Chine* included a description of ceremonial offerings of tea in Tibetan lamaseries. Huc noted that there were two types of "tea session"—the "special tea" given by a pilgrim for a small group of lamas, and the "general tea" that might be offered to over four thousand people gathered for a major celebration, thereby costing the generous donor a fortune. "On the appointed day of the offering of general tea . . . forty young *chabis,* chosen at random, went to the large kitchen and reappeared a moment later carrying large jars of tea with milk. They moved through the rows, and as they advanced the lamas drew their wooden bowls from their breasts. These were then filled to the brim.

When Alexandra David-Neel first arrived in India, she noted that "near the port was a pavilion where one could take tea, excellent tea, with toast, cakes and other products of English culinary art." *L'Inde où j'ai vécu.* India imitated this British ritual, modifying it to accommodate local traditions and even adopting certain Tibetan customs (such as steeping the leaves in milk). *Above:* On the Pakistani border, Indian soldiers drink tea accompanied by spicy pastries called *samosas. Opposite:* A Kashmiri woman takes a break from farm chores to drink tea flavored with cardamom seeds and crushed almonds.

Everyone drank in silence, taking care to draw the corner of a scarf in front of the bowl. This gesture of modesty was an acknowledgment of the unseemliness of this material act, so out of keeping with the holiness of the place. . . . When the celebration was over, the presiding lama solemnly pronounced the name of the pious pilgrim who had obtained the immense merit of entertaining the holy community of lamas."

Tibet is perhaps the only place in the world where tea is considered a sacred offering. Yet it is also an essential element of local hospitality, as in China. A guest will usually be invited to sit at a low table set before the hearth, that center of domestic life. The table will be set with a bowl, a *tsamba* box and sometimes a sort of churn used to mix the butter into the salty tea. To avoid bad luck, bowls must be filled to the brim.

A thousand years separate the ninth-century arrival of Chinese tea in Tibet and the nineteenth-century planting of Chinese tea in India by English colonists. India, notably the Himalayan foothills in the north, was a land highly suited to the cultivation of a shrub that already grew wild in the Assam region. Assam, in fact, produced the first Indian tea, which was sold in London in 1839. Living conditions on those early plantations were appalling, but this of course did not prevent the colonists, British to the bitter end, from religiously observing "tea time."

On steamy verandas overlooking large estates hacked out of the jungle, planters would place pith helmets and canes on the table before ritually drinking their tea in the tepid breeze of a punkah fanned by a servant. Tea was occasionally accompanied by spice buns, cakes and sandwiches.

Now the world's leading producer and number two exporter of tea (just after Ceylon), India is also a major tea-drinking country. Tea is drunk especially in the north, since southern Indians prefer coffee. Tiny tea stalls line the sidewalks of northern cities, where all day long *chayvalas* (tea sellers) serve customers seated on small benches. The carefully brewed *chai* is kept constantly hot in a sort of samovar, and a glass costs only a few rupees. It is usually served very strong, with lots of sugar and milk (often concentrated). Hurried customers often pour a little tea in the saucer to cool it before drinking. As a popular national beverage, tea is also drunk at home, in the city and in the smallest of villages. In the Punjab, to the north, tea is mixed with boiling milk and strong spices.

But anyone who has traveled through India, particularly in the suffocating, dehydrating heat of the monsoon season, has noted and appreciated the wonderful institution of serving tea in trains and stations. It is kept hot in large kettles and served in small clay cups that are shattered after use, thereby assuring travelers that no member of a

"Tea is the beverage of ceremonious peoples, and like the dense monsoon rains, it is both calming and stimulating, encouraging conversation and relaxation. . . . Ideas and traditions steep slowly in its steamy transparence." Pascal Bruckner, *Parias*. *Opposite*: A teapot heating on the burner, next to pepper and red chillies used in the spicy tea of northern India.

lower caste has drunk from the same vessel. In large stations—which in India are like small cities that throb with life day and night—the former "retiring rooms" have been transformed into inexpensive bedrooms. If you stay the night, a boy dressed in white will knock on the door at about six in the morning and announce in a loud voice: "Morning tea! Morning tea!" In this vast country with its changing landscapes, tea is associated with travel, long journeys during which season and climate vary from region to region. In the foothills of the Himalayas, tea braces voyagers against the cold, and its warmth favors human contact. "In my unbroken solitude," wrote P. Bruneton in *En solitaire dans l'Himalaya*, "I learned to take delight in the pleasure afforded by a cup of tea. When I would go in at dusk, the gentle warmth of tea filled me as night closed in around my eyrie. A simple cup of tea has often been the only spark needed to make an acquaintance, inaugurating a bond of friendship that could last a lifetime!"

"Here I am, as usual, comfortably installed in a first-class compartment. This is the sixth train I have taken since arriving in India. . . . If I board at night, an employee waits at the station to indicate the compartment reserved for me; at daybreak, barely have I opened my eyes when I am served *chota-khazri* (that is to say tea, a biscuit and a banana—a sort of appetizer before breakfast)." Ferdinand Goetel, *Voyage aux Indes*, 1937. *Above:* A hawker carries his utensils in the monsoon-flooded streets of Porbandar. *Opposite:* Serving tea on an Indian train sometimes resembles a highwire act more than room service, since the vestibule between the restaurant car and the first-class carriages is locked to prevent other passengers from importuning first-class travelers.

TO MEDITERRANEAN SHORES

Prior to the sixteenth-century discovery of maritime routes linking Europe to Asia, the taste for tea spread west very slowly, in the wake of caravans. Yet it probably reached Afghanistan, that hub of major trade routes (notably the famous silk route), at an early date, and to this day tea remains the country's national beverage. Afghans squat or sit cross-legged as they drink it at home or in *chaikhana* (local tea houses that are sometimes open-air affairs). Tradesmen, pilgrims, camel-drivers, and caravan travelers drink

In following caravan routes westward, the taste for tea evolved according to local customs. West Asian tea drinkers nevertheless share certain traits, notably the use of a samovar. This utensil was supposedly invented at the end of the eighteenth century by Ural metalsmiths, and has become inextricably linked to Russian tea, even though it is also used by Iranians and Afghans. *Above:* Women gathered around a samovar, Persia, nineteenth century. *Opposite:* A tea dealer's stand in Afghanistan, late nineteenth century.

either green tea (*chai sabz*) for its thirst-quenching properties or black tea (*chai siyah*) when they want to warm themselves. They usually add lots of refined sugar, a symbol of wealth. Itinerant hawkers with samovars, stoves and comely teapots aligned on planks of wood also provide steaming tea to travelers along the roadside, occasionally sheltering under large tents of yak hide.

Chaikhana are exuberant, working-class places, and singers and musicians sometimes perform there. People come to chat, to discuss the latest village news, or to pass the time after work. Customers take off their shoes before sitting on mats or large, colorful rugs. Framed prints of Persian calligraphy line the walls, as do floral paintings that echo the patterns painted on the front of the house. Such images evoke springtime and the earth's fertility. Tea is served in round teapots of Risner porcelain imported from the former Soviet Union. But the recent war in Afghanistan, by halting Soviet imports, has led to a small industry in which Afghans carefully imitate the blue cover, red or blue band, and floral patterns invariably found on the original Russian models.

"Seated on a mat and drinking tea from porcelain bowls," wrote Ella Maillart in *La Voie cruelle*, "we admired the mountains toward which we were headed, then the amber fields surrounding the village. . . . Behind us, a row of round teapots gleamed softly in the recess of a shelf, while a boy fanned the charcoal under his samovar."

Caravans eventually brought tea to Mediterranean shores, reaching the Ottoman Empire and Egypt several centuries before it arrived in Western Europe. Contrary to popular belief, Turkey consumes less coffee than tea, which it grows and even exports. Pierre Loti discovered the pleasure of Turkish tea in sweltering Istanbul, where households keep tea constantly on the fire, adding hot water just before serving. This custom is so important to domestic life that mothers, before marrying off their sons, make sure that the future wife is fully conversant in *demilikaçay* (preparing tea). Another tradition still observed in Erzurum, near Iran, requires a host to continually refill a guest's glass until this latter places his teaspoon across the glass. This tradition has died out among most of Turkey's tea houses, or *çayevi*, where tea is served in small, round glasses that fit snugly into the hand, warming it during the cold winter months.

Egypt is Africa's largest consumer of tea and the world's fifth biggest importer (after the United Kingdom, the Commonwealth of Independent States, the United States and Pakistan). Egyptians are truly passionate about tea. This passion weighs heavily on a steep balance of payments deficit, but the government must nevertheless subsidize tea in the same way that it subsidizes

"The souks open. The dark alcoves of the boutiques slowly appear. Tea merchants line up tray after tray. The delicate, chiseled designs of these trays glint in the light above the shoulders of agile carriers who bring them, bowl-laden, to the house. Yet I am struck by the number of consumers who go outside for nourishment; the desire to chat draws them out. I like these colorful drinking establishments. The owner oversees the huge copper kettles that boil and grumble. With a free hand, he wipes tiny glasses with a cloth that is used for everything." F. Balson, *De Kaboul au golfe Persique*, 1949. *Opposite:* A tea merchant's stall on the southern route through Afghanistan, between Kabul and Bamiyan, 1968.

bread, sugar and oil, in order to maintain domestic peace. Tea is everywhere in Egypt—in homes and at the workplace, where it would be unthinkable to go through a day without sipping at least three or four glasses. This taste for tea goes back a long way (tea was drunk regularly at the sultan's court in the fifteenth century) and has reached every corner of the country. In September 1942, Rommel purchased the support of sheikhs at the Siwa oasis in the middle of the Libyan desert by offering them ten thousand Italian lire—and six pounds of tea. Egyptians generally drink a Dust-type tea from India or Ceylon, fairly strong and very sweet but without milk. In the numerous cafés in towns and villages, which often have no soft drinks to offer, customers are brought a glass of unsugared *chai* on a small pewter tray, accompanied by a glass of cold water, a small glass of sugar, a spoon and, on rare occasions, a third glass containing mint leaves. As in many other countries, tea is offered to every visitor to the home, whether stranger, friend or relation. In the houses of fellahs, it is drunk seated on mats placed on the ground. Tea and water—from the Nile—are heated together in a metal teapot placed on an oil stove. The tea is poured

once into the glasses to warm them, then poured back into the teapot and finally into the glasses again.

Contrary to widespread belief, Islamic law does not forbid Muslims to drink black tea on the grounds that it is a fermented beverage. Most Islamic countries, including Egypt, Pakistan and Saudi Arabia, import and consume black tea from India or Ceylon. It would seem that the two main Islamic consumers of green tea—Morocco and Afghanistan—merely reflect local traditions and tastes. In Morocco, green tea is always used because it has become part and parcel of their traditional mint tea. This is nevertheless a recent tradition, since it dates back only to the mid-nineteenth century when British tea merchants, losing their Slavic market as a result of the Crimean War, sought new outlets. Moroccans welcomed tea with delight, for it cut the harshness of their usual brew of mint leaves alone. And they probably preferred green tea because it went well with the color and taste of mint. Moroccan tea is served in small glasses often painted with colorful designs, placed on a round tray of silver, silver-plate, or brass. Tea drinkers sit on long, fringed carpets. As in many Muslim countries, serving tea is a man's affair,

"Presently she returned, carrying an earthen pot of bright coals. While she was boiling the water and preparing the tea, Smaïl chatted with her . . . [and couldn't help but] marvel at the delicate movements of her nimble, henna-stained fingers as she tore the stalks of mint apart and stuffed them into the little teapot." Paul Bowles, *The Sheltering Sky*, 1949. *Above:* Mint tea on an oasis in southern Morocco. *Right:* A gilded, enameled teapot of Moorish design, displayed at the 1851 Universal Exhibition. *Opposite:* Tea in a private home in Fez, Morocco.

and is usually performed by the head of the family, thus symbolizing his role as husband, father, and host. The host uses two different teapots, pouring three successive glasses, from weakest to strongest, holding the teapot high above the glass to create a small head of foam on the tea. Mint tea is served at all hours of the day, accompanied by sweets. It is also drunk during meals, which are rather heavy and spicy, since it eases digestion. Indeed, Moroccans like to say that tea should be bitter as death, sweet as life, and as mellow as love.

THE LAND OF SAMOVARS

Imperial Russia discovered tea in 1638, when the ambassador Vassily Starkov deliv-

Tea time in a *chaikhana* in Kirghizia: "On summer evenings, the *chaikhana* is packed with people. Customers are seated both inside and on the outdoor terrace, its walls adorned with Kirghiz decorations and its carved roof held up by little columns. Roses scent the air. At this time of evening, the statue of Lenin stands out distinctly against the railing, his face turned toward the mountains." V. Vitkovich, *Allons voir la Kirghizie. Above:* A *chaikhana* in Kirghizia. *Preceding double page:* An Afghan *chaikhana.*

ered a Mongol prince's gift of one hundred and forty pounds of tea to Czar Mikhail Fedorovich. Although tea met with immediate success at court, it took two hundred years for it to become a common drink in the land of vodka. For until the eighteenth century, tea arrived from China by caravan, and was available only in a few cities. Moscow boasted the most connoisseurs, to the extent that Muscovites were long called "water drinkers."

Czar Alexander traveled with a large supply of tea when he visited Paris in 1814. He thereby introduced the French to "Russian tea" (which is, in fact, lightly smoked China tea). It quickly became popular in Parisian salons and society circles. In 1843, when Balzac was staying in Saint Petersburg (where he met Madame Hanska), the writer made a point of buying a great deal of what was then considered the finest tea available (not to be confused with the modern "Imperial Russian" blend of India, Ceylon and China teas scented with bergamot and other citrus flavors).

Tea was common throughout the Russian empire by the mid-nineteenth century, having been carried from market to market, even to the remotest of villages. The Rus-

sian word for "tip" comes from *na chai*, "for the tea." The spread of tea was accompanied by the invention of the samovar, which swiftly became a veritable institution imitated the world over. A samovar is a large recipient usually made of copper or bronze (though it also exists in other materials, from porcelain to gold), designed to keep water hot all day long with its charcoal-heated hot-air system. It is topped by a small teapot filled with *tscheinik*, a form of concentrated tea. A samovar also has a small spigot for adding water directly to cups or glasses. Tea-lovers leave the samovar bubbling—or "growling like a storm"—in their sitting room all day long. All great Russian authors, from Dostoevksi to Tolstoy and Gorky, have written about the warm intimacy created by a samovar. It can, however, sometimes disrupt an entire household, as Chekov amusingly described in *Uncle Vanya*: "At night, the professor read and wrote, and often, at around two o'clock in the morning, the bell would ring. . . . What's going on, children? Tea! Everyone had to be awakened to bring him the samovar. . . ."

These days, the Trans-Siberian railroad places a samovar at the disposal of travelers, who are allowed to

"I will provide a few details on what the Russians normally eat. Let's start with beverages. Rich Russians drink real [French] champagne . . . they drink the finest vintages of Bordeaux and Burgundy wines, to which they add various liqueurs produced all over the world. But since wine is very expensive in Russia, small merchants, employees and the common people drink tea during meals." Olympe Audouard, *Voyage aux pays des Boyards*, 1881. *Above:* Russian peasants around the family table, circa 1900.

"He strongly insisted that Velchaninov . . . gulp down two or three cups of light tea. Without asking Velchaninov's permission, he ran to awaken Maura, and helped her to build a fire in the long-neglected kitchen, and boil some water in the samovar. . . . Twenty minutes later the tea was ready." Dostoevsky, "The Eternal Husband." *Above:* The traditional samovar in the kitchen of a nineteenth-century farmer's cabin. *Opposite:* A tea service that reportedly belonged to Czar Nicolas II.

bring their own tea. In every train station, a large kettle called a *kipjatok* provides hot water for a kopek. Russians drink both green and black tea, without milk, often in glasses with a metal handle. They eat a piece of unrefined sugar or a spoonful of fruit jam, which melts in the mouth when mixed with a sip of strong, bitter tea. "Ecstasy," wrote Pushkin, "is a glass full of tea and a piece of sugar in the mouth. . . . "

The former Soviet Union is now one of the main tea-producing regions in the world.

Yet domestic demand is still not met. And, the intensive, mechanized plantations in the newly independent republic of Georgia produce only a relatively poor quality of tea. Russia therefore imports tea from India and Ceylon for the urban middle classes as well as for privileged civil servants.

It is said that the finest harvests of "noble" tea placed on auction at the Colombo and Calcutta exchanges are almost always bought up by Russian importers, for whom tea is a priceless commodity.

"The use of tea is so widespread in Russia that, at a single café-restaurant in Moscow which I will describe later, thirty-three pounds of tea is consumed on an average day, which makes nine hundred ninety pounds per month, or eleven thousand eight hundred eighty pounds per year!" Jacques Boucher de Perthes, *Voyage en Russie*, 1859. *Above:* Taking tea at Margarita's, a famous café in a Moscow park that has become the favorite haunt of Moscow youth. *Opposite, top:* A collection of nineteenth-century samovars in a country home near Moscow. *Opposite, bottom:* An early twentieth-century samovar in brass.

TEA AT GOETHE'S

Tea arrived in Germany by way of Holland, around 1640. It was long considered a medicinal plant and was used mostly by women, who would purchase it at the fashionable herbalist shops that were forerunners to today's pharmacies. But tea had become a part of everyday life by the end of the eighteenth century—in 1772, sixty types of tea were available on the German market, imported from China by the Royal Tea Company (founded 1752) via the ports of Hamburg and Bremen. It could even be taken in one of the magnificent gold- or silver-decorated china tea services produced by porcelain works in Meissen, Bayreuth and Ansbach.

It was around this time that Germans replaced their morning bowl of soup with tea. Soon they were drinking three or four cups a day. In the mid-nineteenth century, Germans adopted the English craze for "punch," a mixture of rum, brandy, sugar, lemon and tea, even though purists considered it a sacrilege to smother tea with alcohol. A little later, consumers acquired a taste for black teas, and by 1880 twenty percent of German imports came from India and Ceylon.

Tea became an indispensable element of high-society salons and artistic circles during the nineteenth century. The way in which it was served was sometimes even interpreted in amorous terms—a bit of froth on the surface of the liquid could represent the promise of a

It was at Meissen in Germany that the secret of how to manufacture china porcelain was finally discovered in 1709. The first tea services made in Europe were based on Chinese models. As in China, cups had no handles. Saucers were deep, without ridges, like a shallow bowl—and the cooling tea was sometimes drunk directly from it. *Above:* A painting by Jacob Denner, 1737, titled *Balthasar Denner and Family.* On the table is a tea urn instead of a Chinese-style teapot. *Opposite:* A portrait by Johann Heinrich Tischbein of his fiancée, painted in 1756. Here, the urn in the foreground contained hot water for tea.

love letter, or even a kiss. "They were seated around a table, drinking tea and talking of love," wrote the poet Heinrich Heine. Goethe believed a tea party was the perfect way to receive friends. In October 1823, his secretary, Eckermann, noted in what was to become the *Interviews* that "this evening I was invited to tea at Goethe's. I greatly enjoyed the company, very natural and casual; some were seated, others were standing, we joked and laughed. Goethe would go from one to the other and he seemed to take greater pleasure in letting his friends talk and listening to them, than in saying something himself. Frau Goethe entered several times, to hug and kiss him." Goethe, in fact, had just married his mistress, Christiane Vulpius, mother of his illegitimate son August. The highly proper ladies of the Weimar Society hesitated to receive her. It was

Fraulein Göchlausen who finally made a decision: "If Goethe gave her his name, we can at least give her a cup of tea!"

Heinrich Heine wrote his famous poem on tea at one of Berlin's literary and artistic gathering spots, the Stehelysh tea and pastry shop. Painters, writers, actors and diplomats would meet there over a cup of tea, in the company of Rahel Varnhagen (Goethe's "darling child") and Henriette Herz (said to be the most beautiful woman in Berlin). The novelist Theodore Fontane was another regular, and Prince Ludwig-Ferdinand could be seen there on occasion with the charming Pauline Wiesel.

During the late nineteenth century—a period marked by an interest in Japanese art and by *Jugendstil*, the German Art Nouveau movement—tea was favored over coffee by the sensitive, sentimental younger generation,

The fashion for things Chinese, which had gripped all of Europe by the seventeenth century, also had an effect on landscape art. Pinnacled temples and pagodas sprang up in parks and gardens, as did tea houses. European tea houses were only distantly related to the Chinese original, but the idea was exotic and China tea was consumed there. *Above:* One of the finest existing examples of these tea houses can be seen in the gardens of the Sans Soucis château in Potsdam. It was built in the eighteenth century by Frederick II of Prussia. *Opposite:* The decoration and sculptures adorning the façade of this delightful pavilion offer a whimsical view of the Orient. *Left:* A gilded porcelain teapot manufactured in Meissen, circa 1725.

who found it more in keeping with the mildly melancholic mood of the day. In the 1920s, on the other hand, German youth was enthusiastic about revolutionary Russia, and it drank "Russian tea" during all-night discussions on how to change the world. Several years later, Germany acquired the European penchant for "tea dances." Grand hotels transformed their bars into ballrooms where all generations would mix on the dance floor between cups of tea. Slang expressions from those years include "let the tea steep" (meaning "forget it") and "tea kettle" (to describe "a clod").

Today it is Hamburg merchants—dynamic businessmen and heirs to a long tradition of trading in tea—who control a large part of the international tea market, surpassing even London in terms of quality. The average German now drinks two or three times as much tea as a Frenchman, and some Germans—notably those in East Friesland near the Dutch border—even consume as much as the English. Frisians, in fact, were the first Germans to adopt tea, and fishermen along the coast used to drink a strong blend of Assam and Java tea mixed with rum. Even if this lusty cocktail is no longer popular, residents of East Friesland still like to drink tea during meals and throughout the day. A little fresh cream is sometimes added to the brew. In summer, tea is drunk iced, to the great delight of children.

"When [von Aschenbach] entered the breakfast-room it was empty. Guests came in while he sat waiting for his order to be filled. As he sipped his tea he saw the Polish girls enter with their governess, chaste and morning-fresh, with sleep-reddened eyelids." Thomas Mann, *Death in Venice*, 1911. *Above:* A book of musical scores for tea dances, 1935. *Opposite, top:* A lithograph by Koch entitled *The Bachelor's Visit*, 1880. *Opposite, bottom:* A 1902 print captioned, "At tea time, women should be taken for what they are." Based on a watercolor by Oscar Bluhm.

Scenes of "Dutch tea" showing how highly the Dutch valued tea kettles (felt in other European countries to be inelegant and impractical). *Above:* A handsome tea salon, a room specially set aside for this purpose in seventeenth-century Dutch homes, and a depiction of a tea-drinker on Delft faïence. *Opposite:* In the eighteenth century, when Nicolas Muys executed this painting, the Dutch had become accustomed to drinking large quantities of tea—Montesquieu wrote in his *Voyage en Hollande* that he was amazed to see a mistress of the house drink thirty cups at a single sitting! *Following double page:* A photograph by Carl Rensing of a Dutch family at tea time, circa 1850.

TEA AND SCONES

Tea is more than just a tradition for the English—it is a way of life. The average Briton drinks six cups of tea per day. In the seventeenth and eighteenth centuries, the advent of tea—like the spread of industry—represented a revolution. As a sign of good taste and a mark of conviviality, it swiftly became an integral part of British society at all levels, significantly changing people's daily life insofar as the day became organized around "tea time." Taking tea was both a working-class and aristocratic affair, becoming highly codified and extremely refined in sophisticated homes. Probably nowhere else in the world has a beverage so pleasantly governed the day of an entire nation.

Handles on cups did not become popular until the end of the eighteenth century. The idea of a handle was supposedly borrowed from the mugs in which the English drank hot wine and beer. By freeing themselves from the Chinese model, European tea services could then evolve toward a wide variety of forms. British factories strove to be ingenious, even producing "mustache cups" with an inner ridge designed to keep elegant mustaches dry. *Above:* Taking tea in England, circa 1740. *Opposite: A Gentleman at Breakfast*, circa 1775, attributed to Henry Walton.

It is perhaps best symbolized by the "early morning cuppa" sipped in bed on awakening, prior to washing and dressing. Each day is thus inaugurated under the sign of tea. As Cecil Roth recounted, "I was recently the guest of Baron Alfred de Rothschild in his Seamore Place palace. Early in the morning, a liveried servant entered my room pushing a huge table on wheels. He asked, 'Would you like tea or a peach, sir?' I chose tea, which immediately provoked another question. 'China, India, or Ceylon, sir?' When I asked for India tea, he enquired, 'With lemon, cream, or milk, sir?' I opted for milk, but he wanted to know which breed of cow I preferred: 'Jersey, Hereford or Sorthorn, sir?' Never had I drunk such a good cup of tea." The "early morning cuppa" is obviously to be followed by an English breakfast of porridge, fish, scrambled or fried eggs and bacon, all washed down by more tea. Such a breakfast is a far cry from the sugary "continental breakfast" eaten in Europe's Latin countries.

The first public sale of tea in England took place in 1657, during Cromwell's stewardship. Trader Thomas Garraway vaunted the drink's numerous medicinal properties. It was swiftly adopted by the cream of London

"Five o'clock tea," served on a low table laid with small sandwiches and light pastries, is quite distinct from "high tea," a solid working-class meal eaten at the family table and constituting the main repast of the day for laborers back from field or factory. *Above:* A photograph taken by William Henry Fox Talbot in 1840, *The Breakfast Table.* This is the first photograph taken of an English tea service. *Opposite:* An 1874 painting titled *Reading the News* by James Tissot, a French artist who lived in London and often included a tea table in his compositions.

society. Women would often withdraw to a sitting room after dinner to drink tea, while the men remained at the table with their port. Thanks to the success of coffee houses, where tea could be procured, the lower classes also had relatively early access to the beverage. In 1660, Samuel Pepys wrote in his diary: "I did send for a cup of tee (a China drinke) of which I had never drank before." The spectacular rise of tea in England was linked to the success of coffee houses, the first of which opened in London in 1652. Fifty years later the capital boasted no fewer than five hundred coffee houses. These establishments became the unrivaled social centers of English life in the seventeenth and eighteenth centuries, for here customers could drink tea, coffee, brandy or rum, and sample a range of delicacies, all the while perusing British and continental newspapers or casually chatting. Apparently, it was here that the European version of tipping was

Despite the unpredictability of English weather, drinking tea outdoors has always been considered an ideal way to pass the time. During the warmer months, some events are intimately bound up with the practice of taking tea on the lawn. Buckingham Palace garden parties, Henley regattas, cricket matches and village festivals all provide an opportunity to sample tea, sandwiches and cakes under large tents specially erected for the occasion. *Above:* Ladies in a garden, Loughton, 1908. *Opposite:* Taking tea on the lawn, photographed by Mortimer around 1900.

born—customers could toss a coin into a box marked T.I.P. ("To Insure Promptness").

In 1706, Thomas Twining, then a young salesman for a London tea merchant, founded "Tom's Coffee House," the first such establishment to specialize in tea. He thus launched what was to become one of the most famous tea rooms in the world. As recounted above, Twining opened a retail shop, The Golden Lyon, eleven years later. This was where women, who were not admitted to coffee houses, could buy and drink their tea. Throughout the eighteenth century, the consumption of tea rose sharply. Fifteen times as much tea was drunk at the close of the century as at the outset. In the final fifteen years alone, consumption doubled as the habit of drinking tea filtered down from the

Like their parents, the children of good Edwardian families were highly attached to the ritual of taking tea, associated as it was with sweets and the security of nursery life. J. M. Barrie's story *Peter Pan* demonstrates that budding Britons prefer tea time to the marvelous universe of an enchanted isle: "'Do you want an adventure now,' Peter said casually to John, 'or would you like to have your tea first?' Wendy said, 'Tea first,' quickly." J. M. Barrie, *Peter Pan*, 1904. *Above: A Cheerful Giver*, by Fred Morgan, circa 1900.

aristocracy to the middle and lower classes. The swift spread of tea was linked to a sharp cut in the tea tax ordained by Pitt in 1783, an attempt to undermine an increasingly well-organized black market that profited from a commerce employing over forty thousand people and three hundred ships.

The craze for tea during the latter half of the century had already led to the creation of "tea gardens." England revived the art of landscape gardening by abandoning French formalism to celebrate nature in all its romantic forms. Londoners from all walks of life could enjoy refined gardens at Ranelagh, Marylebone, and Vauxhall. There, in a Gainsborough-like setting where the baroque competed with the classical, strollers could sit on a patch of grass or around a table, not far from a rococo temple or the remnant of a column. They might hear the strains of an orchestra as they sipped a cup of tea, accompanied by bread, butter, or cake, or even a tasty combination of a morsel between two slices of bread, recently invented by the clever Lord John Sandwich.

It was during the Victorian era that "lunch"—a midday meal enabling men to get together at the club and women to meet at home—took on greater importance. Slowly, eating times and habits changed. Dinner took place at seven or eight o'clock instead of five or six, so that the supper normally eaten at ten at night became superfluous. It was in 1840 that Anna, seventh duchess of Bedford, invented "afternoon tea" to be taken at home at four o'clock (the appointed hour becoming five o'clock early in the twentieth century). This was a way to quell the inevitable hunger pangs between lunch and dinner, and became so popular among affluent classes that it not only provoked the decline of tea gardens but became one of the mainstays of the British way of life.

Afternoon tea was taken before a fire in the drawing room in winter, but might be enjoyed in the shade of a tree in the garden during summer. It represented an agreeable if strictly regulated marriage of good taste, refinement and sociability. One dressed comfortably yet elegantly, and full, light "tea gowns" (simpler and less tightly cinched at the waist than ordinary gowns) were created in the 1880s. A fine tablecloth and china or silver tea service were also required;

"Ten minutes later, they were sitting downstairs in the comfortable kitchen being introduced to Curtis, a rather gruff-looking, grey-haired old man, and being regaled with strong tea, bread and butter, Devonshire cream and hard-boiled eggs. While they ate and drank they listened. Within half an hour they knew everything there was to be known about the inhabitants of the small community." Agatha Christie, *The Sittaford Mystery*, 1931. *Above:* A 1930 Empire Marketing Board poster titled *And We'll All Have Tea.*

this would include a teapot, milk pitcher, sugar bowl, several tightly sealed tea caddies, twelve cups, saucers, plates and caddy spoons. Finally, and above all, the mistress of the house had to be expert in preparing the tea and the light meal that went with it. Naturally, it was in the best of taste to have everything served by a domestic or, even better, by the young lady of the house who could thereby demonstrate the savoir-faire and refinement needed to enter society. She must, for instance, pour milk into the cup prior to pouring the tea; the tea itself must come from India or Ceylon, which produced the only two types of tea considered proper.

Right from the start, the buffet meal accompanying afternoon tea was systematized once and for all. Guests were entitled to small cucumber, tomato, egg or watercress sandwiches, or toast with cinnamon, almond biscuits, scones, jam (usually strawberry), various pound and sponge cakes. Soon "cream teas" became fashionable, the tea being accompanied by freshly clotted cream. Children, who were served tea in the nursery in the Victorian and Edwardian periods, were notably allowed to have sandwiches made with sardines, chocolate or bananas, or perhaps muffins

and crumpets with jellies and jams, as well as all sorts of sweet or savory cakes. Naturally enough, little girls would sit their dolls around a miniature tea service.

In the countryside, afternoon tea was taken on returning from the fields, and therefore became the main meal of the day. In many cottages and farms, where hospitality was the rule, it was not unusual to see a sign over the doorway inviting travelers or even vagabonds to come in for a cup of tea with scones, buns or home-made bacon pie.

Local traditions sprang up in all corners of the kingdom, from clotted cream in Devon, to eggs and conserves in the west country, to apple cake in Dorset. In Cornwall, the use of sugar was banned the day Methodist preacher John Wesley recommended boycotting it as a way of discouraging slavery in the West Indies.

In "elegant and polite" country homes, tea would be taken either in a small drawing room or the veranda or garden arbor, depending on the season. Tea might be drunk from Stafford porcelain during endless bridge parties, or between two innings of cricket, sets of tennis, or games of croquet. Iced tea and sandwiches

Three British versions of tea time. *Above:* The spare Welsh style. *Opposite, top:* A Rene Mackintosh interior for the recently restored Glasgow tea rooms founded by Miss Cranston, the temperance crusader. *Opposite, bottom:* A 1925 tea room that continues to fulfill Londoners' rural yearnings—this "Tea House at College Farm" is still located on a small farm in north London.

soon became a popular treat during the hottest days of summer.

Among the middle and lower urban classes, four o'clock tea also became more than a simple break, evolving into a substantial meal of sandwiches made of meat, fish, pâté or cheese. If they were unable to take tea at home, modest Londoners would flock to the tea houses that flourished in the wake of the amazing success of A.B.C. tea rooms.

The Aerated Bread Company had launched its tea rooms in 1864. Women were allowed to enter unaccompanied, and such tea houses soon took over from the tea gardens.

Queen Victoria could hardly find fault with this, for she officially instituted tea time at Buckingham Palace. As an adolescent, Victoria had been obliged to bend to the somewhat fanatical will of her governess, the duchess of Northumberland, who was

By the nineteenth century, Britons considered tea an essential element of daily well-being, and subsequently linked it to the social health of the country. *Above:* In 1946, when the government promised that the standard of living would improve, railway travelers saw ultra-modern tea trolleys appear in train stations. *Opposite:* In a Welsh county where the unemployment rate hit 90 percent in some towns in 1935, an event was organized to offer tea to disadvantaged children, not unlike the "tea moralities" of the Victorian era.

"'What tea do you drink?' asked Wyatt. 'I don't know anything about tea. Told Abdul to get some. Thought that girl might like to come in to tea one day. Darned pretty girl. Must do something for her. She must be bored to death in a place like this. . . .'" Agatha Christie, *The Sittaford Mystery*, 1931. *Above:* London, 1949. *Opposite:* Afternoon tea in Torquay, a tourist stop in southern England, 1954.

convinced of the diabolical effects of two highly fashionable activities—reading *The Times* and drinking tea. Victoria respectfully obeyed until 1838, the year of her coronation. Directly after the ceremony, the young queen took a deep breath, then asked for the latest *Times* and a cup of tea. Liveried servants carried out her orders instantly. "Now I know that I truly reign," she is reported to have said. Tea remained one of the queen's two favorite beverages. The other was whisky.

Throughout her sixty-four-year reign, Victoria supported "Tea Moralities," tea parties organized by charitable societies on behalf of underprivileged groups such as the unemployed, the homeless, and prostitutes. A comforting cup of tea, offered with the approval of God and queen, was also supposed to encourage a new habit among popula-

tions ravaged by alcoholism. The wretchedness of London's poor was evoked by Charles Dickens with humor and tenderness in his description of the melancholy cheer of Christmas so dear to the English. "The blended scents of tea and coffee were so grateful to the nose," he wrote in *A Christmas Carol*, " . . . the raisins were so plentiful and rare, the almonds so extremely white . . . the candied fruits so caked and spotted with molten sugar as to make the coldest lookers-on feel faint. . . . " Another tradition sprang up as the industrial revolution spread: the tea break, a mid-morning and mid-afternoon pause enabling staff and workers to drink a cup of tea and have a snack. But it was not until unions fought for the right to a tea break around 1820 that this practice, so energetically resisted by employers in the

Above: The prince of Wales sampling Cameroon tea. *Opposite:* A 1950 painting by Sir James Gunn showing the royal family of England taking tea at Windsor Castle. Every afternoon, King George VI, his wife Elizabeth and the two young princesses assembled around a cup of tea accompanied by watercress sandwiches, kirsch-flavored cake or coffee éclairs. Today, the current monarch, Elizabeth II, concludes all business and returns to her apartments at five o'clock sharp—tea time. The tea comes from Twinings, the china from Worcester, and the queen uses these precious moments to meet with her children or look after her pet corgis.

name of productivity, became the rule.

Like many other tea-related traditions, this twice-daily break is on the decline in Britain. Office hours, new technology, the mass arrival of women in the labor force and new dietary concerns have considerably altered eating and drinking habits. Automatic drink dispensers have transformed the break into a swizzling of some wretched concoction—perched on the corner of the desk—at no particular time of day. The tradition of "high tea," a veritable evening meal composed of cold meat, scrambled eggs and bacon, salad, cakes and fruit, as well as the ubiquitous cup of tea, is now observed only in the rural north of England and in Scotland.

In London, the most delectable and refined afternoon tea is served in the tea rooms of grand hotels. Take, for example, the menu proposed by Brown's Hotel for five o'clock tea: in addition to an excellent selection of teas (including their own blend and a green tea), the menu lists a variety of small sandwiches, toast and jam, scones and clotted cream, cakes and the chef's own pastries. *Above:* Tea in a suite at Claridge's. *Opposite:* Brown's tea service, with afternoon tea menus from the Waldorf, the Ritz, the Savoy and Brown's, on a sheet featuring designs of eighteenth-century Minton china.

Should one want to indulge in the full ritual of "afternoon tea," this is generally done in the salon of one of the grand hotels, unless one is lucky enough to be invited to tea by the queen or a member of the gentry. The ceremony duly takes place every day at the Waldorf, the Ritz, the Savoy and Brown's. In the Palm Court at the Ritz, for instance, with its plush setting that combines Louis XVI design with Art Deco, carefully muted lighting gives customers the pleasant impression of being cut off from the world, far from the bustle of Piccadilly. The chimerical atmosphere is enhanced by palm trees and a fountain adorned with mermaids and tritons contemplated by a languid nymph. An impeccably trained staff sets china tea services on marble tables, serving Darjeeling or Earl Grey to a clientele that dresses for the occasion. Customers may partake of time-honored varieties of finger sandwiches prepared by a famous "sandwich chef." The cucumber, cream cheese and smoked salmon sandwiches are made with dark bread, whereas the smoked ham, egg salad and watercress and cheddar sandwiches are served on white. Then come deliciously fresh scones, accompanied by cream and strawberry jam, and finally cakes and petits fours.

Even if the nature and ritual of "afternoon tea" have been considerably simplified in recent years, it remains a special and often indispensable part of the day for the British. What Paul Morand wrote in *Le Nouveau Londres* still applies to modern England. "To say, at about five o'clock, 'I haven't yet had tea,' can upset an entire household; complete strangers practically feel obliged to offer you 'a nice cup of tea'—from Ceylon, naturally, even though ever since the island gained its independence tea is also grown in Argentina and the Azores."

"The cup of tea on arrival at a country house is a thing which, as a rule, I particularly enjoy. I like the crackling logs, the shaded lights, the scent of buttered toast, the general atmosphere of leisured cosiness." P. G. Wodehouse, *The Code of the Woosters. Above:* A Scottish silver tea service. *Opposite:* In a traditional Scottish manor, the table is set for afternoon tea.

FROM THE BOSTON TEA PARTY TO INSTANT TEA

As might be expected, English immigrants to America took "tea time" with them. Tea was introduced into North America as early as the seventeenth century by the Dutch, and its consumption became more widespread in the following century, particularly among the upper classes who so enjoyed tea parties. Such parties, with their silver teapots and porcelain tea services, became the symbol of social success, occasions at which the elite families of Philadelphia and Boston would meet. Soon, however, tea was also drunk in less affluent circles, becoming a universal sign of good manners and hospitality. In New York, the Chatham Street pump was thought to provide the best water for tea. "Tea-water men" hawked it loudly through the streets of the city. In the early eighteenth century, Puritans drank bitter tea with butter and salt, whereas most New Englanders preferred green China tea scented with saffron, iris root or gardenia petals. Such habits waned over the decades, but tea continued to be a popular beverage. By the end of the eighteenth century, a third of the colonies' population drank it twice a day.

Tea was thus the third-ranking colonial import during the 1760s, behind textiles and manufactured goods. When England found itself financially strapped by the French and Indian War, it levied a heavy tax on tea. Throughout the colonies, the tea tax provoked violent patriotic reaction and calls for

Two years after the Boston Tea Party, it was a silversmith by the name of Paul Revere (known for his silver teapots) who determined the outcome of the first battle between the English and the Americans at Lexington. On the night of 18 April 1775, Revere climbed the stairs of the highest steeple in Boston, carrying two lanterns to signal the American patriots of the arrival of British troops—"one if by land, two if by sea." From that point onward, Revere changed the design of his teapots, abandoning his rococo style to invent a "patriotic teapot." Its sober, pure, neoclassic design symbolized democratic values. *Opposite:* Portrait of Paul Revere by John Singleton Copley. *Above:* A painting by Johann Eckstein (1736-1817) titled *The Samuels Family*.

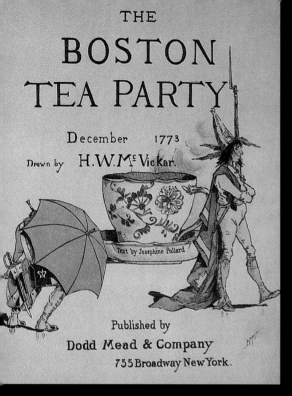

THE
BOSTON
TEA PARTY

December 1773

Drawn by H.W. McVickar.

Text by Josephine Pollard

Published by
Dodd Mead & Company
755 Broadway New York.

AND A MEETING WAS HELD, WHERE THE PROCLAMATION
WAS READ, THAT HAD CAUSED ALL THIS PERTURBATION.

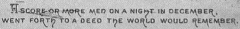

A SCORE OR MORE MEN ON A NIGHT IN DECEMBER,
WENT FORTH TO A DEED THE WORLD WOULD REMEMBER.

HE WAS READY TO BURST WITH RAGE NO DOUBT,
WHEN THE CLERK IN A LOUD VOICE READ ABOUT

a boycott. An alarmed East India Company had the tax lowered, but this was not enough to cool tempers. On 16 December 1773, patriots from Saint Andrew's masonic lodge in Boston dressed up as Mohawk Indians and boarded three of the company's ships. They threw three hundred and forty chests of tea into the harbor. The incident became ironically known as the "Boston Tea Party," and unleashed English reprisals. But such action merely triggered other tea parties, ultimately leading to the battle of Bunker Hill and the Declaration of Independence in 1776. Tea had indeed started a revolution.

In the late eighteenth century, the young American merchant fleet entered the tea trade by going straight to the source—China. Imports of tea then rose spectacularly, going from six hundred tons in 1790 to ten times that amount in 1825. Numerous New England fortunes were built on this trade, money that was subsequently invested in local textile mills. In the face of a wave of new immigrants from Europe and Asia, the affluent classes in New England clung to the time-honored English traditions. Tea, along with hunting, became a social ritual designed to indicate membership in a privileged group. At the same time, tea became highly prized by the grand southern planters, and during the American civil war "blockade runners" supplied plantations with tea worth its weight in gold.

Oliver Wendell Holmes (1809-1894) wrote in his *Ballad of the Boston Tea Party:*

The waters in the rebel bay
Have kept the tea-leaf savor;
Our old North-Enders in their spray
Still taste a Hyson flavor;

And freedom's teacup still o'erflows
With ever-fresh libations,
To cheat of slumber all her foes
And cheer the wakening nations!

Above and opposite: Excerpts from a commemorative album published in New York in 1882. *Below:* Stamps issued for the bicentenary of the Boston Tea Party.

In the early twentieth century, a New York tea merchant named Thomas Sullivan had the bright idea of manufacturing tiny bags of silk containing a single dose of tea. This invention met with immediate and long-lasting success, radically changing the art of preparing tea and leading, alas, to the production of poor-quality tea better suited to being crushed and packed in bags. At roughly the same time, in 1904, tea dealer Richard Blechynden went to the Saint Louis World's Fair to introduce Americans to black tea from India, which until then was an unknown commodity. But the summer weather was sweltering, and visitors were not inclined to rush to Blechynden's stand to drink a hot cup of tea. Though thirsty, Blechynden himself shrank from the idea. So he put two ice cubes in a glass and poured the tea over them. Iced tea was born. Many fair-goers refreshed themselves with the new drink, and iced tea soon spread throughout the southern states.

Americans still drink a great deal of iced tea, often with lemon and sugar, sometimes with a dash of rum. This has led to a booming trade in "instant tea," a freeze-dried powder to be dissolved in cold water. Needless to say, tea connoisseurs do not think much of the product. Americans increasingly drink ready-made tea sold in cans, thereby significantly altering "tea consciousness" in their country. Without such initiatives, however, the United States (a country that consumes five times as much coffee as tea-based beverages) would certainly not be the world's third-largest importer of tea.

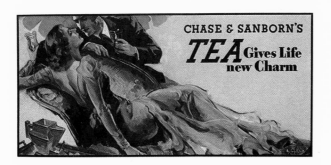

"Make up a good fire in the library, please, and bring the tea up . . . after rearranging her dark hair before the mirror, [she] carefully dressed herself in a loose garment of velvet and lace which lay awaiting her on the sofa. . . . She had been one of the first women in New York to have tea every afternoon at five o'clock, and to put off her walking-dress for a tea-gown." Edith Wharton, *New Year's Day*, 1923. *Above:* American advertising image. *Opposite:* *Tea Leaves*, a 1909 painting by the American artist W. Paxton depicting the practice of attempting to read the future in tea leaves. *Preceding double page:* Tea time in New England, circa 1900.

FRENCH SAVOIR-FAIRE

By the end of the 1630s, tea was already being appreciated in several small Parisian social circles, having been introduced at court by Cardinal Mazarin, who took it for his gout. As in most other countries, therefore, tea won its first French converts due to its medicinal properties. In the second half of the seventeenth century, scholarly books abounded in which tea's often controversial merits were vaunted and compared to those of other new products such as coffee and chocolate. In the France of that time, knowledge of both medicine and tea were far from having reached the degree of sophistication found in China, and as late as 1692 a certain François Massialot advocated "smoking tea like tobacco, after having lightly dampened the leaves with a dew-like sprinkling of brandy; also, the sediment or ashes remaining in the bowl of the pipe is marvelous for whitening the teeth."

Things exotic were highly fashionable. So when the *Amphitrite*, the first French ship to return from China, unloaded its costly cargo in 1700, moneyed *précieuses* (ostentatiously stylish women) were able to procure tea as well as silks, screens, lacquers, porcelain, rhubarb, and camphor. The beverage made from the Chinese plant became more widespread in high society during the reign of Louis XIV, when it was considered a pleasant and convivial refreshment beneficial even to the healthy. But Paris salons remained divided between advocates and detractors, and tea became an excellent subject of

The habit of putting milk in tea reportedly started in France. Madame de Sévigné described how Madame de la Sablière launched the fashion: "Madame de la Sablière took her tea with milk, as she told me the other day, because it was to her taste." In fact, there was a practical reason for this custom—pouring a little cold milk in the cup prevented the scalding tea from cracking fragile porcelain from China. This is apparently behind the English insistence on "M.I.F." ("milk in first"). *Above: Woman Taking Tea, by J. B. S. Chardin. Opposite: Toilette, by François Boucher, 1742. Preceding double page: English Tea in Paris, at the Prince de Conti's Court, with the young Mozart at the harpsichord, by Olivier Barthelemy, 1766.*

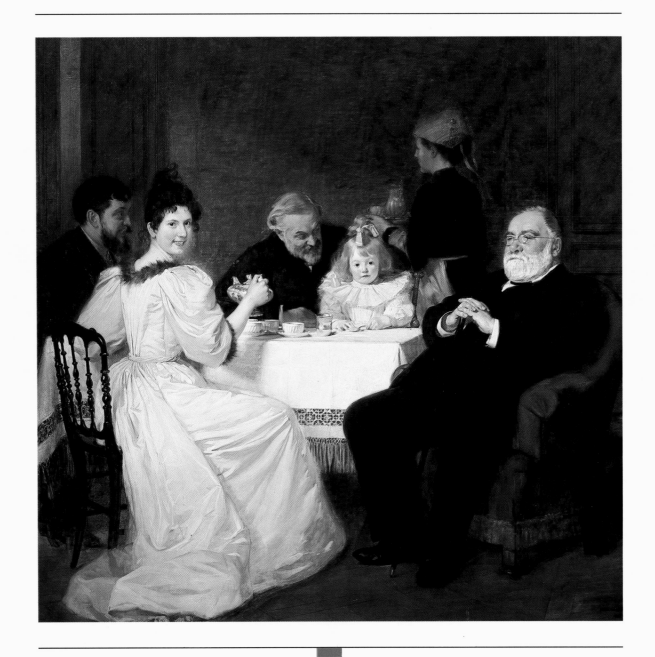

Unlike the British, the French have never considered tea, which is a stimulant, suitable for children. In spite of these reservations, however, generations of little girls have received miniature tea services as a gift. "Your Aunt D'Aubert instructed me to give you this little tea set as a gift from her. . . . The delighted Sophie took the tray with its six cups, teapot, silver sugar bowl and creamer." Comtesse de Ségur, *Les Malheurs de Sophie. Above: Francisque Sarcex at the Home of Adolphe Brisson's Daughter*, by M. A. Baschet. *Opposite: The Cup of Tea*, by M. A. Baschet, 1896. In 1925 Maurice Ravel directed a French child to drink tea on stage, in *L'Enfant et les sortilèges*.

conversation. The marquise de Sévigné, a great supporter of tea, witnessed some serious tea-drinking: "Saw the princesse de Tarente . . . who takes twelve cups of tea every day . . . which, she says, cures all her ills. She assured me that Monsieur le Landgrave drank forty cups every morning. 'But Madame, perhaps it is really only thirty or so.' 'No, forty. He was dying, and it brought him back to life before our eyes.'" Nicolas Audiger, author of *La Maison Réglée* (The Well-Ordered Household), added that tea "is normally taken in the morning to awaken the mind and stimulate the appetite." This opinion, however, was not completely shared by a vivacious princess of the Palatinate. "Tea is not as necessary for Protestant ministers as for Catholic priests who cannot marry," she claimed, "because it makes one chaste."

In France, tea remained rarer and much more expensive than coffee for a long time. Moreover, it was associated with costly utensils of porcelain and silver, unlike coffee which was soon being hawked in the streets and offered in the new, popular establishments known as cafés. By 1715, Paris boasted nearly three hundred of them. Tea was therefore the prerogative of wealthy families, a sign of utmost distinction, and an opportunity for the finest silversmiths and potters from the Vincennes and Sèvres factories to exercise their talent. Tea was perhaps too heavily marked by its Parisian, aristocratic beginnings to become a truly popular beverage in France. It was not until the nineteenth century that the new bourgeoisie and provincial gentry dared taste it, albeit gingerly. In *Illusions Perdues*, the tea-loving Balzac described a woman from Angoulême who "loudly informed the entire province of an evening

In France, tea rooms—as distinct from cafés—were for a long time the only public place that women could frequent without endangering their reputations. In her *Mémoires d'une jeune fille rangée*, Simone de Beauvoir recalled how college youths from good families would take her to tea in the back rooms of bakery shops, rather than in the tea salons that were too expensive for students. "They did not frequent cafés, and in any case would never have taken girls there." *Above:* Teapots in the Grand Hôtel de Cabourg. *Opposite:* The Fauchon tea rooms in Paris in 1910, and packets of tea formerly used by Mariage Frères tea dealers.

party of ice cream, cake and tea, a great innovation in a city where tea was still sold at apothecaries as a remedy for indigestion." During this very period, the British were drinking tea six times a day, from Buckingham Palace to the Liverpool slums.

By the end of the nineteenth century, however, thanks to "tea salons" and "tea dances," the beverage had become fairly common in sophisticated circles. Seaside resorts, with their casinos, flower-studded verandas and grand hotels such as the Hôtel du Palais in Biarritz and the Grand Hôtel in Cabourg, provided the perfect occasion to take tea with Proustian languor, letting conversation drift along pleasantly. The Bois de Boulogne near Paris also offered arbor-shaded tables at the Bagatelle, to which one could be conspicuously driven by landau.

France can at least pride itself on having invented the *salon de thé*, or fancy tea room so rare in an England where fine tea can now be had only in a grand hotel. Such salons have flourished in Paris since the early twentieth century, like the establishment founded in 1903 by Antoine Rumpelmeyer, a confectioner of Viennese origin; now known as Angelina, the tea room is still popular today. Faithful to the traditionally elitist connotations of tea in France, these salons are the opposite of noisy, working-class bistros, and they enable connoisseurs to savor fine teas in peace and comfort—indeed, intimacy—in surroundings unmarked by the march of time. Unlike cafés (those perfect symbols of French conviviality, the preferred meeting place of artists and intellectuals), tea rooms were long thought to be "tepid, draft-proof homes for old people," in Roland Jaccard's words. And it is true that their often old-fashioned charm is more

353. PARIS — Bois de Boulogne
Le Restaurant de la Cascade C. M.

"Odette poured Swann 'his' tea and asked, 'Milk or lemon?' And since he answered, 'Milk,' she laughingly said, 'A drop!' and then, since he found it good, 'So you see that I know what you like.' That tea, in fact, seemed like a precious thing to Swann, and . . . during the entire trip back in his coupé . . . he repeated to himself, 'It would be jolly pleasant to have a little lady at whose place one could find that ever so rare thing, good tea.'" Marcel Proust, *Un amour de Swann. Above:* Tea time at the Restaurant de la Cascade in the Bois de Boulogne, circa 1900. *Opposite:* A 1908 painting by G. Croegaert titled *In Private.*

conducive to melancholy and reverie than to social mingling and debate.

Yet this image is swiftly changing today, for France is one of the few countries in which the consumption of tea continues to grow—in fact it has doubled in the past thirty years. Every neighborhood in Paris, as well as the downtown area of every provincial city, boasts new and inviting tea rooms that are less strait-laced than their predecessors, thereby attracting an increasingly younger clientele. The French have always been interested in exploring exotic flavors, and by tradition they expect authentic, high-quality gastronomy. The better tea rooms thus enable them to discover an infinite variety of teas. And French retailers now offer these new gourmets what is perhaps the widest range of refined blends

"The day I noted down a conversation with Vincent that I had so enjoyed, we had gone for tea near Saint-Séverin, to the English pub that has such good lemon pies. It wasn't to reward him, for he in no way deserved it. It was because we wanted quite simply to talk. Vincent was eleven years old." In this excerpt from *La Maison de papier*, F. Mallet-Joris is referring to the Tea Caddy, the most British of Paris tea rooms. *Above:* Other Parisian tea salons include Le Loir dans la Théière and Les Contes de Thés. *Opposite:* The interior decor at Angelina has been officially listed as being of historic interest.

and scented teas in the world. Customers today flock to certain Parisian tea shops to buy a few of the three hundred teas listed in the catalogue, all sold in bulk so that they can be sniffed prior to purchase (unless, of course, the customer prefers cotton muslin teabags in which even excellent teas can steep in dignity). In such shops, all blends are composed of the finest harvests, and only natural essences are used to scent flavored teas.

French savoir-faire in tea has thus become synonymous with strict standards and quality, and is now being exported along with champagne and haute couture. Strange signs of the times include seeing a member of the British royal family in the London branch of a French tea merchant, and witnessing customers in Tokyo department stores flock to buy "French tea."

Today, tea is under pressure from the massive invasion of soft drinks. Industrial manufacturers of tea, responding to the new soft-drink habits, have stressed over the past twenty years the sale of teabags and, to a lesser extent, powdered instant and ready-made teas. This concession to modern life-style has spurred several countries such as Indonesia to sacrifice its fine harvest in favor of a poorer quality of mass-produced tea. On the other hand, choosing not to fight on the Coca-Cola front, many tea merchants, particularly those in France, have decided to help a growing number of consumers discover and appreciate all the subtlety of the precious nectar. The success of this approach means that demand for quality teas now outstrips supply, once again encouraging tea-growing countries to carefully cultivate their gardens. Thus, even if the continued rise in the consumption of tea is due to mass-produced goods, it is thanks to the revival of an art that a growing number of connoisseurs are acquiring the true savoir-faire associated with tea time.

French enthusiasm for tea goes beyond fine tea shops and salons. Silversmiths and leather craftsmen also contribute to the French concept of tea as an *art de vivre*. Elegant wicker baskets complete with thermos and full tea service brought picnic teas back into fashion. *Above:* The Vuitton firm designed this travel case for taking tea in style anywhere. In the 1880s, the Christofle company offered an exclusive blend of smoky China tea to buyers of a new line of silver teaware inlaid with ebony. *Opposite:* Jean-Louis Dumas-Hermès, a paragon of Parisian elegance, sips his favorite tea from a Limoges china cup.

THE TASTE

· OF TEA ·

Catherine Donzel

"English tea or China tea?" This is the question Asian waiters invariably ask of European tourists sitting, say, in the early-morning shade of a large green and white awning on the terrace of the Raffles Hotel in Singapore, or beneath the gilded stucco decorating the lobby of the Peninsula Hotel in Hong Kong. If travelers opt for the first choice, breakfast will be served with rather strong black tea, probably from Ceylon, in a teabag. Since it will have steeped too long in the teapot, milk will have to be added to mask the bitterness. Yet if guests choose "China tea" out of curiosity, they may well note a bemused glint in the waiter's eye. The hotel employee knows full well that Western tourists will probably be surprised by the tea they have just ordered. For instance, it might turn out to be a semifermented whole-leaf tea known as Oolong, a pale brew with a refreshing and flowery flavor. Some disconcerted Westerners may then attempt, unsuccessfully, to evoke a more familiar flavor by adding milk and sugar. This is heresy in the eyes of the Chinese waiter, who will nevertheless refrain from voicing his disapproval of the all-too-common faux pas. Yet such ignorance is comparable to that of rich Asians who spoil fine cognac by adding fizzy water.

For decades, Western tea drinkers have marched to a British tune. Previously, of course, people knew that numerous varieties of tea existed, and that each had its own special taste. In the late seventeenth century, Europe drank green tea, the first kind to be imported. One hundred years later, all of Europe from Saint Petersburg to Paris delighted in the sweet and aromatic flavor of black China teas, avidly consuming "flowery teas" and "scented teas."

Elsewhere, subsequently famous teas such as the "caravan tea" carried across the Gobi desert from China into Russia initially seduced generations of connoisseurs thanks to its marked flavor of adventure. Starting in 1850, however, Western tastes in tea became progressively standardized, and only a few refined and curious palates managed to hold out against uniformity. England began growing tea in its colonies and eventually established a monopoly over the tea trade, ultimately managing to impose its own criteria on the rest of the Western world—the only tea worthy of the name was henceforth the strong, robust, deep amber variety from Ceylon or Assam. Major British firms marketed this perfectly uniform product on

"Nowhere is the English genius of domesticity more notably evidenced than in the festival of afternoon tea," declared George Gissing (1857-1903) in *The Private Papers of Henry Ryecroft*. "One of the shining moments of my day is that when, having returned a little weary from an afternoon walk, I exchange boots for slippers, out-of-doors coat for easy, familiar, shabby jacket, and, in my deep, soft-elbowed chair, await the tea-tray. . . ." *Above:* Late nineteenth-century French metal tea container with raised painted design. *Opposite:* Early morning tea served at an inn in the Cotswolds, England. *Page 196:* Preparing cups of tea for a professional tasting session at the London Centre of the Tea Trade.

an international scale. They did this so thoroughly that many Westerners considered these strong blends of India teas to be the only valid point of reference. This opinion is still held by many people today, even though it completely disregards the rich universe of tea. When one realizes that there are more kinds of tea in China than there are wines in France, that each local plot of land produces a tea unlike any other, that the flavor of Darjeeling changes as the seasons change, and that the bud and open leaf on any given tea branch have differing properties, one begins to realize why it is such a shame to cling to a narrow view of tea.

Openly exploring the wide range of flavors produced by teas from India, Japan, China and Africa, however, requires a great deal of care and discrimination. There is not only a tea for every taste, but also for every moment of the day. Some outstanding teas can be compared to great vintage wines, whereas other perfectly worthy yet more conventional teas are to be drunk daily like decent table wines. This is why white tea, one of the most exclusive varieties in the world, should really be tasted only if one is already a connoisseur. To a less experienced palate, the crystal-clear liquid made from these pretty, velvety buds will simply appear bland—an expensive mistake to make, given the price of white tea!

Similarly, people accustomed to strong, full-bodied teas have to adapt gradually to green or semifermented teas with delicate, subtle flavors. At first, for instance, a spoonful or two of such teas can be added to a normal blend, or they can be sampled with food chosen to enhance their character. It would seem, moreover, that consumers follow this

Until the Second World War, most of the European tea trade passed not only through London but also Amsterdam, which boasted a major auction center. Currently, continental Europe buys much of its international supply of tea in Hamburg. During the auctions that still govern 75 percent of the tea trade, buy orders depend entirely on tea tasters. They must work swiftly as well as accurately, since the quality of the shipments is judged by samples tasted just prior to auction. *Above:* A professional tasting session in Hamburg. *Opposite:* A tea merchant in Kurseong, Bengal.

progressive initiation almost naturally. In France, for example, the scented teas that were in vogue in the 1970s produced a new generation of connoisseurs. Scented teas are in fact an ideal starting point because they familiarize tea drinkers with both standard and exotic flavors, and then lead bit by bit to an interest in more refined aromas. Tea drinkers evolve almost unconsciously from a taste for flowers and fruit to a taste for tea.

The tea leaf itself bears the traits of the soil in which it was grown. Each harvest has its own special quality, whether cultivated on the plains, in the mountains, on Himalayan slopes in springtime or in Ceylon during a hot summer. Each cup of tea represents an imaginary voyage. The names of the various regions alone conjure up distant lands, and the names of gardens are even more evocative. It is probable that many customers occasionally purchase one tea rather than another simply because of the exotic, enchanting appeal of the name on one of those large, painted tins lining the retailer's shelves. Good tea merchants are obviously aware of this effect, for they shrewdly invent attractive names for house blends and newly imported varieties.

In China, the practice of numbering the main types of tea is used for foreigners only, since merchants employ an anthology of poetic and picturesque names to entice local consumers. China tea is rarely labeled only by province or place of origin. The countless varieties of China tea are named after flowers, rivers, mythological heroes and celestial divinities, not to mention the all-powerful Black Dragon clan so popular in "the land of ten thousand teas."

Magical-sounding names constitute one of the charms of drinking tea. But they can also be a source of error and confusion for less experienced aficionados. Before wandering into the maze of gardens and pluckings (a field that requires solid bearings), it is better to decide exactly what pleasure or stimulation is being sought from a cup of tea. Breakfast normally calls for a strong, full-bodied tea, whereas a light, digestive variety is a better way to round off lunch. A refreshing, vitamin-rich drink may serve as a thirst-quencher throughout the day, while a mild, scented, low-theine tea is ideal in the evening. Indeed, there are teas for all seasons. One need merely become familiar with the major categories defined by European tasters to

Above: Yorkshire is the English county perhaps most attached to British tea-drinking traditions. "High tea" there might include smoked fish and soft-boiled eggs. *Left:* High-handled Chinese teapots. Similarly shaped vessels were also used in China to pour wine. *Opposite:* The "Tee Import" shop in Basel, Switzerland, and its current owner. The establishment was founded in the eighteenth century by an importer of china porcelain, becoming Switzerland's first tea shop.

identify the various characteristics of black, green and semifermented teas.

Well before Westerners decided to bring a little order to the cluttered world of tea, the Chinese had already established the broad outlines of their own classification system. The Chinese system is based essentially on the color of the liquor—red, green, white or yellow. It requires such

sophisticated knowledge of tea that it was never adopted by Europeans. In the West, teas were classified solely by country of origin (India, China, Ceylon, et cetera) until roughly 1945. Indicating the place of origin, however, is not sufficient to describe the flavor of a tea. Many tea rooms in France, for instance, list "China tea" on the menu. This is meaningless in itself, and simply indicates that the term "China" now refers only to smoky teas from the Fujian region, thereby obscuring the fact that China also produces unsmoked black teas, semifermented teas, and a wide range of green teas. "Ceylon" and "Assam" are also the object of rather hasty generalizations. These strong and stimulating morning teas can sometimes be quite delicate and thus appropriate for a soothing cup of afternoon tea. The difference is found in the leaf—that is to say, whether the leaves are whole or broken.

That is why Western experts have employed a new classification system for the past fifty years, a system that takes the degree of fermentation into account, along with manufacturing processes and the "grade" of the tea as determined by the size and form of the leaves. Taken together, these criteria constitute a rich palette of specific flavors, enabling tea drinkers to choose their variety according to taste or mood.

In describing the characteristics of tea, professional tasters employ a vocabulary as picturesque as that used by wine-tasters. Thus a tea leaf with fine appearance is "well-twisted"; if too large for the grade to which it is assigned, it is described as "bold." An immature tea tastes "green," whereas a fully "mature" tea is neither bitter nor flat. *Top:* A member of the U.S. Board of Tea Experts in a tasting session in New York, 1940. *Above:* A china cup, an English teapot, and a Chinese tea container. *Opposite:* Teas lining the shelves of the Mariage Frères boutique in Paris.

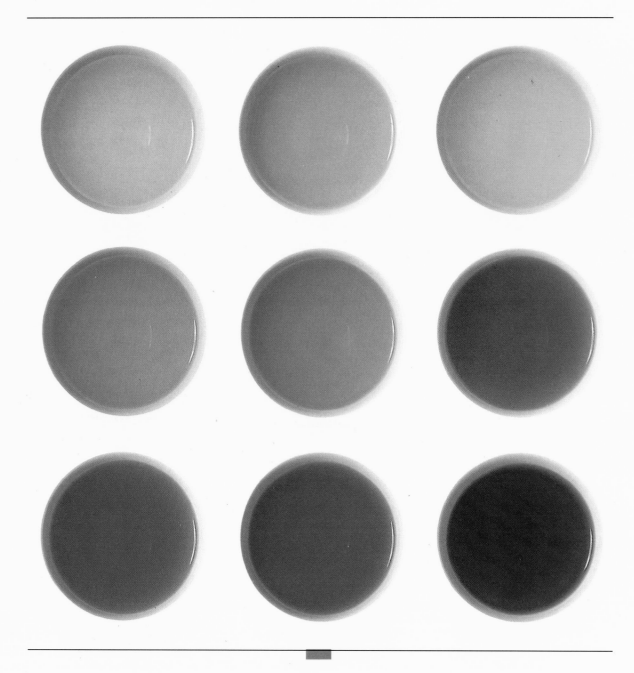

"Relatives were invited to sample the teas. . . . They began with the most delicate teas, the China teas that retain a subtle scent of lacquer, the almost colorless teas from Formosa with their flowery taste, the somewhat orangey Orange Pekoes, and the subtle Russian teas. . . . " Jacques Chardonne, *Les Destinées sentimentales. Above, left to right, top to bottom:* The color of tea—Yin Zhen (white China tea), Lung Ching (green China tea), Sencha Honyama (green Japan tea), Ti Kuan Yin (semifermented Formosa tea), T.G.F.O.P. "first flush" Darjeeling, Ceylon Orange Pekoe, Darjeeling Broken Pekoe Souchong, Uva Highlands B.O.P. (Ceylon), B.O.P. Fannings (Cameroon).

COLOR AND FLAVOR

According to legend, black tea was produced by chance, in the hold of an East India Company ship transporting green China tea that accidently fermented during the crossing. Whereupon Europeans, immediately attracted to the aroma of the fortuitous product, convinced the Chinese to manufacture this new type of tea. The anecdote obviously has no basis in fact, but it accurately conveys the truth that black tea is a typically Western taste that appeals less to an Oriental palate, which is traditionally more sensitive to the subtle aromas of green and semifermented teas. For that matter, black tea is mass produced only in those countries where Westerners themselves planted the crop—India, Ceylon, and Africa. Japan produces no fermented tea, and China exports almost all of its black tea.

Europeans acquired a taste for black tea along with the taste for sweets. The full, round aroma of **black tea** married very well, in fact, with sweet flavors; moreover, it was the only tea that could tolerate—on occasion—a drop of milk. As to the golden brown color of black tea, it naturally appealed to people accustomed to admiring the red, maroon and ochre hues of wine and beer. These colors were more familiar to Europeans than the pale pink or jade green of Oriental brews.

Once beyond such generalizations, however, it quickly becomes clear that not all black teas are alike. The secret of their diversity is encoded in several obscure initials usually written just after the country of origin. Thus B.O.P., G.F.O.P. or even F.T.G.F.O.P. seen in a catalogue or on a container simply indicates the degree of maturity and the form of the tea leaf.

Among whole-leaf black teas, the most subtle quality is called Flowery Orange Pekoe (F.O.P.). It refers to teas harvested early and carefully, composed only of unopened buds and the first two leaves beneath the bud. The word Pekoe comes from the Chinese *Pak-ho*, which alludes to the fine hair of a newborn infant and, by association, was applied to young tea buds still covered with a light down. "Orange," contrary to popular belief, has nothing to do with color or flavor, but refers to the princes of Orange descended from the house of Nassau—it thus conveys the idea of noble quality and was probably first used by Dutch merchants. The leaves of a Flowery Orange Pekoe are easily identifiable and highly attractive. They are finely rolled lengthwise and interspersed with the golden tips of the buds. The more tips there are, the more expensive the tea. The grades of excellence move up through Golden Flowery Orange Pekoe (G.F.O.P.) to Finest Tippy Golden Flowery Orange Pekoe (F.T.G.F.O.P), yielding light, clear teas

"Tea is drunk to forget the din of the world," wrote Chinese sage T'ien Yiheng. *Following double page:* Tea utensils in modern-day China. (1) Lined basket for keeping the teapot warm. (2) Tea service dating from the beginning of this century. (3) Semifermented jasmine tea. (4) Pewter tea caddy. (5-6-8) Sundry packages of semifermented tea, including (7) a metal tin. (9-11) Round cakes of compressed tea. (10) A caddy from the Fook Ming Tong shop in Hong Kong.

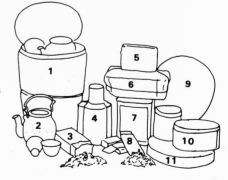

composed almost entirely of tips. This type of leaf, wherever it comes from, will never produce a very strong brew; to the contrary, it makes an extremely fine and aromatic drink. Depending on the time of harvest—notably in Darjeeling—it may display a subtlety comparable to the great semifermented teas. Flowery Orange Pekoe is an ideal afternoon tea, as is Orange Pekoe (O.P.), which is the product of an equally careful but somewhat later harvest. At this stage of growth, the tea no longer has light tips and the leaves are longer and more elegant.

There are other sorts of whole-leaf black teas issued from less fine plucking methods, but they are not usually sold as such. Thus Pekoe, which is the product of the third leaf on the branch, is generally used in blends. Souchong, with dark leaves that are large and thick, is used in smoky teas such as Lapsang Souchong and Tarry Souchong.

For the strength and tannic acid taste usually sought in an early-morning cup of tea, a brew made from broken leaves is more appropriate. Contrary to common belief, broken-leaf teas are not necessarily inferior to whole-leaf teas. They have simply undergone a transformation process designed to make the tea stronger.

The finest broken-leaf teas, Broken Orange Pekoe, are made from high-quality harvests and may contain golden tips when made from Flowery Orange Pekoe. Such teas can be quite expensive, for they may require fairly sophisticated manufacturing processes.

Teas labeled "Dust" or "Fannings" are made of crushed leaves, and produce an even stronger beverage with greater body. These teas are usually sold in teabags, for they consist of tiny pieces of leaf.

Broken-leaf, dust and fannings can withstand a drop of milk and a little sugar—should the tea-drinker insist on them.

Green tea is worlds away from black tea. Dark liquors and the taste of tannic acid give way to pale hues and refreshing aromas as the scene shifts from European dining tables to Buddhist temples. Sugary tea parties and robust breakfasts have been left far behind. The classification system so well adapted to Western tastes is of no use in the East. In the land of green tea, the concepts of body and strength are not relevant, and the various "grades" of leaf (which, in the case of black tea, indicate relative strength) have little meaning. For that matter, with the exception of a powdered green tea produced in Japan ("Matcha"), unfermented teas are always whole-leaf teas. Those sold in the West are usually the product of the finest harvests. Local techniques of cultivation and manufacture, on the other hand, yield a wide variety of aromas. Thus green teas from China and Formosa are strikingly different from the teas produced according to Japanese methods.

"Even as the difference in favorite vintages marks the separate idiosyncracies of different periods and nationalities of Europe, so the Tea-ideals characterize their various moods of Oriental culture." Kakuzo Okakura, *The Book of Tea. Opposite:* Japanese tea merchants choosing teas offered by an American firm doing business in Japan. This selection probably involves black tea, since Japan, which exports only a little green tea, imports a sizable amount of fermented tea.

Better-quality China teas are generally sold as flat leaves of a fine verdigris color, or silvery in the case of superior teas such as Dong Yang Dong Bai, composed exclusively of downy buds and very young leaves. The color of the liquid itself is crystalline, varying from orange-green to pale pink. The taste is mild and subtle. The leaves of other qualities of tea, less prized by the Chinese, are carefully rolled into a ball. Hyson, for example, a green tea drunk widely during the nineteenth century, is rolled into fine pearls; gunpowder, on the other hand, is rolled into larger, regular balls (this is the variety that is mixed with fresh mint to make the mint tea drunk in Muslim countries).

Japan produces only green tea, of which there are numerous varieties. Only a few kinds are exported, however, the rest being consumed locally. These unusually refreshing teas superbly recreate the organic harmony of the gardens in which they were grown. Japanese tea leaves are greener and more vivid in color than China tea, and the liquor is stronger in hue, going from jade green to light yellow. The taste evokes the aromatic strength of freshly cut herbs. Westerners are generally surprised by Japanese tea. It requires an educated palate to savor the rare delights of Gyokuro ("Precious Dew"), whose buds, three weeks prior to plucking, are shielded by a large black canvas, an operation designed to increase their chlorophyll content and intensify their dark green hue. Similarly, experience is required to truly appreciate a grand Matcha Uji, which comes in the form of a jade-green powder that is whipped in a little pure water and yields a magnificent, concentrated, nourishing beverage. It is more sensible to begin by sampling Sencha teas, which are excellent yet less sophisticated than the previous two. Bancha teas are also a good place to start, since they are produced for everyday use in Japan, not unlike European table wines.

A green tea is judged on its aroma, which must be highly developed, and on the length of its taste in the mouth. Great Japanese teas are recognizable from the way they fill the palate with an enduring, fragrant, slightly sweet flavor. Green tea sometimes tends to be bitter. This may be considered a drawback by some, even though the bitter taste—which is one of the features of tea in general—is often highly appreciated. Whatever the case, the bitterness can be eliminated by rinsing green tea in water prior to steeping. Unfermented teas must be drunk straight, without milk or sugar. They make a pleasant accompaniment to a meal, thanks to their digestive properties. They are gentle teas that can be drunk throughout the day; given their high vitamin C content, however, they are not recommended in the evening. Although not an excitant, green teas have a revitalizing effect and are

"When all is complete deep in the teapot, when tea, mint, and sugar have completely diffused throughout the water, coloring and saturating it . . . then a glass will be filled and poured back into the mixture, blending it further. Then comes waiting. Motionless waiting. Finally, from high up, like some green cataract whose sight and sound mesmerize, the tea will once again cascade into a glass. Now it can be drunk, dreamily, forehead bowed, fingers held wide away from the scalding glass." Simone Jacquemard, *Le mariage berbère. Opposite:* Mint tea and oriental pastries.

also reputed to be an intellectual stimulant.

A tea leaf should "have creases like leathern boot of Tatar horsemen, curl like the dewlap of a mighty bullock, unfold like a mist rising out of a ravine." This image of the ideal leaf is taken from Kakuzo Okakura's translation of Lu Yu's seventh-century *Chaking*, the bible of tea. It is a good description of **semifermented teas**. Bulky, always whole and never rolled, such tea comes in a vast range of extravagant forms—the wiry coil of the legendary dragon, the quick-frozen flight of an insect, the angry arch of the eyebrow of a Chinese actor (one semifermented tea even draws its name from this visual analogy). Semifermented tea undergoes only an initial fermentation process and therefore combines the aromas of black and green teas. Smoother than black tea, less fresh and grassy than green tea, semifermented tea displays a certain balance and harmony.

Known by the generic name of Oolong, the various types of semifermented tea can be divided into two main groups. One includes the so-called China Oolong teas, rarely exported, that have undergone 12 to 20 percent of the fermentation process. These teas are common in China and have a very "Oriental" taste reminiscent of spring vegetation. They produce a pale yellow liquor. The second major group—Formosa Oolong teas—undergoes longer fermentation (approximately 60 percent) and produces a golden brew with a more "Occidental" flavor. Among the teas of this latter type normally consumed in Europe is one called Oriental Beauty, also known in France as Black Dragon (the literal translation of *Oolong*). This is the most highly prized semifermented tea, as reflected in its price. It is generally described as having a taste of orchids, and is much appreciated by those who prefer Darjeeling and other light, aromatic teas.

Semifermented tea can be drunk throughout the day, and goes well with meals (apart from breakfast, which may require a stronger tea). It is low in theine, and is therefore perfect before bedtime, especially when steeped with jasmine, orange flowers, rose petals or other flowers known to have a calming effect.

Opposite: Afternoon in an indoor garden. The tea is served in Wedgwood china, whose characteristic two-color Greek pattern was designed in the 1830s. *Preceding double page:* (1) Cast-iron Japanese brazier used in the tea ceremony. (2) Ancient Japanese cast-iron kettle. (3) Chinese tea service including a cup with cover (*chung*) used to brew a single cup of tea. (4) Metal tea caddy, 1900. (5) Nineteenth-century tea caddy in brass. (6) Nineteenth-century brass samovar from Russia. (7-8) Packages of China tea. (9) An eighteenth-century merchant's tea container. (10) Tea caddy, early twentieth century. (11) Porcelain tea service from Japan, circa 1900.

HOW TO PREPARE TEA

Knowing how to choose the right tea is not enough. Tea from a great garden, composed of elegant-looking leaves that give off a wonderful aroma, may nevertheless prove to be disappointingly dull in the cup. In fact, it often happens that customers of exclusive tea shops will angrily return to the counter after having bought a superb tea, complaining that the brew did not live up to its promise and that the highly vaunted tea was not good. In most cases, however, it would be truer to say that it was the water or the teapot that was not good, or that the steeping time was wrong. For fully half of the success of tea depends on the care with which it is prepared.

First of all, the teapot—which is the tea-drinker's most precious "tool"—must be appropriate to the task, and be treated with respect. It should never be washed or scrubbed, but simply rinsed with running water and left to dry, uncovered, in the open air. This is designed to retain the deposit of tannin that coats the sides of the teapot little by little, for a natural lining enhances the flavor of tea

brewed in the pot. A highly "seasoned" teapot used for very strong or smoky teas, however, will retain their odor and should therefore not be used for mild, subtle teas. This is why, ideally, a serious tea-drinker should have a different teapot for each type of tea. Short of beginning an extensive teapot collection, however, three will suffice—one for strong tea, one for mild tea, and a third for scented teas. A terracotta or silver-plated teapot is well-suited to strong teas rich in tannin, such as Ceylon and Assam teas. Apparently pewter also gives excellent results for such teas, as does cast iron. Plain cast iron is appreciated by the Japanese because it releases extremely beneficial mineral salts, but it requires special care. Enameled cast iron, on the other hand, like porcelain and fine china, makes an ideal teapot for green and semifermented teas, as well as for light black teas such as Darjeeling. The shape of the teapot is not important, provided that it is functional—the rest is simply a question of personal taste. Perhaps the most practical model is a porcelain teapot with a felt-lined metallic cover; made in England and Germany, it is usually very

"When there weren't many visitors on a Tuesday, tea was served in the sitting room itself. [Countess Sabine] called Vandeuvres over, and questioned him on the way the English made tea. He often went to England, where his horses raced. According to Vandeuvres, only the Russians knew how to make tea, and he gave her the recipe." Emile Zola, *Nana*. *Above:* A photograph by M. Jeziorowska, *Rebeka*. *Opposite:* A collection of teapots and cups in a Moscow apartment. Most of these are Russian, and date from the early nineteenth century.

attractive and offers the advantage of keeping tea at the right temperature for a long time.

It is too often overlooked that, in the final analysis, tea is merely flavored water, and that therefore the quality of the water must be taken into account. It is said that Chinese tea masters were able to recognize the specific water used to brew tea, whether it came from the edge of a river, from the middle of a running torrent, or from a deep well. Some extremely refined connoisseurs have highly reputed water shipped to them, and it is said that the queen of England never travels without a supply of spring water used to prepare her tea. On a more simple level, it is important to be sure that the water is pure, fresh, odorless and free of calcium. In some areas, urban tap water is naturally soft and perfectly appropriate. To check, boil a little water beforehand, then smell the steam to detect any potentially undesirable odors. Or simply use the water filters sold in many stores. A neutral mineral water, for instance one recommended for infants, is another good source.

After having selected teapot and water, it is at last time to brew the tea. First of all, heat water in a kettle preferably used only for preparing tea. The teapot should be thoroughly warmed before the tea leaves are placed in it, being careful to use the right amount. One can generally figure 2.5 grams of tea per cup, which is approximately one rounded teaspoon. This measure applies most accurately to whole, black tea leaves; for broken leaves, a level teaspoon is enough, and for fannings, two-thirds of a teaspoon will suffice. A good cup of Oolong, on the other hand, requires two good spoonfuls of tea leaves. The proper dose for green tea varies according to the type in question; in general, one can reckon on three grams per cup, but the tea merchant's advice is important here.

Once placed in the bottom of the thoroughly heated teapot, the leaves should be left there for a minute or two, wrapped in the ambient steam, for only then will the full aroma be released.

"Dear, do you think the water has boiled enough to be poured over the tea?"

"I think, dearest, that it is still too soon."

Too late is more like it. When Madame de Staël penned this dialogue in *Corinne*, she was apparently unaware that water for tea should never be allowed to boil, for this will make it flat and lifeless. Furthermore, if too hot, it will harm the tea leaves and alter their flavor. The water should be poured on the leaves when it is barely simmering. Everything then becomes a question of time. Black tea should be steeped from three minutes (broken leaves) to five minutes (whole leaves). Semifermented teas require seven minutes to bring out their best flavor. Green tea from Japan is brewed for one or two minutes, whereas China tea requires

"The room was well furnished and scrupulously clean, and there was a wood fire in the grate. Given a chair at a gate-legged table on which the miller's wife spread a spotless, beautifully laundered cloth, Mrs. Bradley gazed out of the window at the denuded trees and the grey autumn sky. Her hostess returned with tea, scones, butter and jam and informed her that 'the girl' was attending to 'the gentleman' in the car." Gladys Mitchell, *The Greenstone Griffins*, 1983. *Opposite, top:* Afternoon tea. *Opposite, bottom:* A commemorative teapot portraying Queen Victoria and Prince Albert. *Following double page:* (1) Solid silver eighteenth-century tea caddy. (2, 4) Tea chests of fine inlaid wood. (5) Traditional British teapot. (6) Chinese bamboo strainer. (3,7) Nineteenth-century household tea caddies made of tin. (8) Early nineteenth-century engraved pewter tea caddy.

three to five minutes, but once again variations exist and the advice of a competent salesperson is useful.

Stir well prior to serving and, above all, remove the leaves once the tea has steeped. Nothing is gained, except added bitterness, from letting the tea brew longer, despite a rather widely held belief that the longer a tea is steeped the more stimulating and rich in theine it will be. This is untrue, for theine is released in the first minute of brewing, after which the increased presence of tannins will tend to counter its effect.

If the teapot has a built-in strainer, simply lift it out to remove the leaves. If not, a strainer made of cotton (the most appropriate material) may be used, to be removed when the tea is ready to serve. Tea balls are also convenient, but must be rather large in order to provide enough space for the tea to swell, since leaves double in volume once plunged into water.

Obviously, it is not always possible to follow every rule to the letter when making a cup of tea. That is no reason, however, to deprive oneself of a good cup of tea at the office, for example. This is where teabags of muslin (not paper!) come in handy. Good tea merchants sell teabags of a quality comparable to loose tea. Unfortunately, it is very difficult to find green and semifermented teas packaged this way.

There is no point in trying to save time by buying a large quantity of tea in advance. It is a fragile and precious commodity, and must be stored in an airtight box or jar, away from dampness and light, for a limited period only—twelve months for black teas, six to

The earliest tea caddies were imported from China and Japan, and were originally simple terracotta jars with a cover used to measure out the tea. Since tea was a costly item in Europe, caddies soon became small chests complete with lock, to which only the mistress of the house held the key. Such caddies normally had two compartments (for green and black tea) plus a dish in which teas could be blended or sugar stored (sugar being another expensive commodity). *Above:* Tea caddies. *Opposite:* English teapots of glazed clay with pewter tops.

"She was a fine woman, a perfect gentlewoman. She had taken life, as she liked a cup of tea—weak, with an exquisite aroma and plenty of cream and sugar." Henry James, "De Grey: A Romance," 1868. *Above:* Two Americans enjoying five o'clock tea in 1930. *Preceding double page:* (1) A 1925 teapot. (2) An infuser. (3) Teaspoons. (4) Tea-flavored jelly. (5) Porcelain infuser for a single cup of tea. (6,7) 1930s-style tea service. (8) Rock sugar. (9) Muslin teabags.

eight months for semifermented and green teas (which the Japanese store in the refrigerator). If tea is purchased in a supermarket, the final sale date should be checked.

There remains the thorny question of milk, sugar and lemon. For "true" connoisseurs, it is a sacrilege to employ such additives. This hard line may be softened, however, to satisfy all tastes.

Thus, as mentioned above, certain teas "tolerate" a drop of cold milk. In general, this applies to the strong, full-bodied black teas in broken-leaf form, such as those from Assam, Ceylon, and Indonesia. In short, it might be said that milk is suitable—perhaps—for morning teas. But for lighter teas of the Darjeeling type, as well as for smoky, green and semifermented teas, milk is absolutely unacceptable. Lemon, which changes both the taste and color of tea, is to be banned in all cases. A thin slice of orange, on the other hand, can sometimes enhance the aroma of an Assam or Ceylon tea.

Sugar, if one insists on adding it, should be neutral white rock sugar (in Britain, "candy" sugar), preferably to be used only in average-quality black tea. It might be pointed out that the flavor of sugar does marry well with scented teas, as they are already a kind of dessert.

Nevertheless, sugar and milk will always encounter staunch opponents, as reflected in a passage from an article by George Orwell in which he claimed that adding sugar to tea was like adding salt or pepper. He compared the natural astringency of tea to the pleasant bitterness of English beer, and pointed out that if one really wanted a sweet drink, the most sensible thing to do would be to melt sugar in hot water. Not everyone's cup of tea!

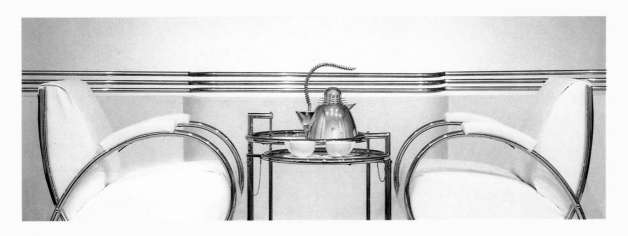

Steeping tea in an elegant teapot and sipping it from a charming cup was long a luxury reserved for the privileged classes. But by the 1850s, the invention of electroplating techniques (which allowed for the infinite reproduction of a metallic object) and the mass production of ceramics put a tea service within reach of most people. Furthermore, this alliance of art and industry has meant that fine tea accessories can be periodically re-manufactured. Thus perfect reproductions of tea services designed for use on glamorous ocean liners or in palaces are now for sale, enabling connoisseurs to add a drop of fantasy to their tea. *Above:* A photograph by Michel Dubois titled *Hollywood 1932*, included in a limited-edition book on tea published at the initiative of Damman Frères.

GREAT TEA REGIONS
AND TRADITIONAL BLENDS

The processing, maturity and form of the leaf give tea its taste—the region in which it was grown gives it its character. Original features associated with each estate mean that all the major classes of tea can be endlessly subdivided and distinguished. Yet some districts produce teas that are inevitably prestigious, thanks to a combination of favorable climate and tried-and-tested cultivation techniques. The most famous of these exclusive teas come from just five countries—Ceylon (Sri Lanka), China, Formosa (Taiwan), India and Japan.

Kitti Cha Sangmanee, expert tea-taster, scours the globe for rare teas and creates exclusive blends for Mariage Frères in Paris.

C e y l o n

Ceylon, that "island of tea," basically produces black tea known for its aromatic amber liquor and its rich, full, astringent flavor. It goes very well with a little cold milk and harmoniously accompanies a sweet breakfast or afternoon pastry. Ceylonese estates all produce a tea of particular flavor but they are too numerous to be listed. It is more useful here to classify the island's tea according to the grades of leaf, progressing from

1 - CEYLON F.O.P.

2 - CEYLON O.P.

3 - CEYLON B.O.P.

4 - KEEMUN F.O.P.

5 - LAPSANG SOUCHONG

the mildest to the strongest. A famous estate or two is listed under each grade.

Flowery Orange Pekoe. Very attractive leaves with golden tips that give a flavorful, mellow brew of great distinction. Estates that produce fine F.O.P.s include Berubeula and Allen Valley. An afternoon tea.

Orange Pekoe. Tea with long, thin leaves, fruitier than F.O.P. The Pettiagalla and Kenilworth estates produce remarkable O.P. tea. An afternoon tea.

Flowery Pekoe. The liquor is both full and aromatic. A well-balanced tea, with fine estates in Dyraaba and Uva Highlands. A morning and afternoon tea.

Broken Orange Pekoe. In this category, teas from Saint James, Dimbula and Uva Highlands are noted for being flavory and full, with great character. A morning tea.

Broken Orange Pekoe Fannings. These teas are so full-bodied that they are a good substitute for coffee. A drop of cold milk, merely tolerated in the above grades, is strongly recommended here, for milk marries marvelously well with fannings. The Uva Highlands and Dyraaba estates produce fine fannings. A morning and after-meal tea.

A young tea picker in Ceylon (Sri Lanka). In her right hand she holds the delicate terminal stem gathered during a "fine plucking"—just two top leaves and the leaf-bud, or "tip."

China

BLACK TEAS FROM CHINA are mild and low in theine, and therefore considered perfect afternoon and evening teas. With the exception of Yunnan, they are never taken with milk or sugar.

Keemun. This type of tea is not smoky, and is known for its orchid aroma and brilliant red liquor. Its mild, sweet flavor makes it a perfect evening tea. It is also frequently used as the base for scented blends.

Lapsang Souchong. This moderately smoky tea is produced by withering the leaves over open fires of pine. It goes well with salty and spicy dishes, and with cheese.

Yunnan. This non-smoky tea comes in G.F.O.P. and T.G.F.O.P grades, and is one of China's "noble" varieties. It is one of the rare teas to combine aroma with strength, subtlety with rich taste. Full and round, it is nicknamed "the mocha of tea." With a fine golden liquor and a taste that remains long in the mouth, Yunnan will tolerate a drop of milk and is perfect for a continental breakfast.

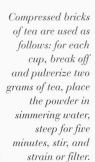

Compressed bricks of tea are used as follows: for each cup, break off and pulverize two grams of tea, place the powder in simmering water, steep for five minutes, stir, and strain or filter.

GREEN CHINA TEA, like that from Japan, should never be drunk with milk or sugar.

Dong Yang Dong Bai. One of the finest green teas in the world, it is noted for its flowery bouquet, its smooth, long-lasting taste and its clear liquor.

6 - YUNNAN T. G. F. O. P.

7 - DONG YANG DONG BAI

8 - LUNG CHING

9 - PI LO CHUN

10 - SILVER DRAGON

Lung Ching ("Dragon Well"). This famous tea yields a superb jade-colored liquor. Its exquisite flavor and delicate aroma are perfect any time of the day, but Lung Ching is particularly appreciated by those who need to stay up late since it is stimulating and is reputed to help keep the mind clear.

Pi Lo Chun ("Spiral of Spring Jade"). A fairly rare tea sold only by the finest tea dealers. Round and mild, it should be saved for grand occasions.

Silver Dragon. This tea owes its name to the silver down covering its leaves, whose shape suggests the silhouette of a dragon. It produces a light, limpid liquor of intense aroma and sweet taste. A daytime tea.

WHITE TEA is different from black, green and semifermented teas. It is difficult to obtain, for production is limited. White tea undergoes almost no transformation—once harvested, it is merely withered and dried. Its name, a literal translation from the Chinese, probably comes from the very pale color of its liquor. Moreover, high-quality white teas come in the form of white buds whose texture is comparable to the petals of the edelweiss flower. The subtle taste of white tea requires an experienced palate already initiated into the "Oriental" flavors of green and semifermented teas.

Yin Zhen ("Silver Needles"). This white tea is produced by the "imperial" plucking method, performed at dawn on only two days of the year. The beauty of its fine, silvery buds, its delicate and refreshing taste make it one of the most glamorous—and expensive—teas in the world. To be sampled, preferably, in summer.

Pai Mu Tan. This has a somewhat more ordinary quality than Yin Zhen, but the leaf can still be appreciated in its natural state, for it remains just as it was when plucked from the bush. Smooth and flowery, this is an appropriate tea for evening.

F o r m o s a

Tarry Souchong. Produced according to traditional Chinese methods, this is the most heavily smoked black tea of all. Reserved for aficionados of its special smoky flavor, Tarry Souchong makes a good accompaniment to hearty breakfasts and brunches.

Gunpowder. This green tea is rolled into little balls that "explode" when placed in the teapot. It is widely used to prepare mint tea, but is also delicious on its own. The yellow-green liquor is highly refreshing. A relaxing, afternoon tea.

SEMIFERMENTED TEAS have become the great specialty of the island of Formosa, where the

11 · YIN ZHEN

12 · PAI MU TAN

13 · TARRY SOUCHONG

14 · GUNPOWDER

15 · IMPERIAL OOLONG

finest of them are produced. Their taste is generally more subtle than that of semifermented teas made in China. They are to be drunk plain, without milk, during or after a meal, at any time of day. They are low in theine and therefore also appropriate as an evening beverage.

Imperial Oolong. This is the finest tea from the family of Oriental Beauty (or Black Dragon) teas. The liquor is somewhat amber-colored and hints of chestnut and honey flavors. Highly aromatic, it is a fine evening tea.

Grand Pouchong. This is one of the family of China Oolongs that has undergone only slight fermentation. The liquor has a fine golden color, the delicate aroma yields a subtle flavor. A daytime or evening tea.

Ti Kuan Yin ("Iron Goddess of Mercy"). This tea is known for its digestive properties. The liquor is amber-hued, and it has a mild taste yet fully developed aroma.

Tung Ting. Another member of the China Oolong family, Tung Ting is one of the most famous Formosa teas. The liquor is orange-red, the flavor very mild. A daytime and evening tea.

Semifermented China tea sold in the form of a round cake of compressed leaves is steeped in small Chinese teapots of red clay.

India

Teas from India, like those from Ceylon, are black teas designed to satisfy "Western" tastes, and are therefore characterized by their full-bodied flavor and rich, deeply colored liquor. But India also produces a wide variety of black teas that are more subtle, and can be as delicate as semifermented teas from China and Formosa. India teas therefore offer a fine initiation into the taste of tea in general.

Assam. These are morning teas par excellence, with a strong, malty taste and dark liquor. They go well with a drop of cold milk. Assam boasts a number of famous gardens, including Thowra, Numalighur and Napuk. Tea drinkers nevertheless have a hard time distinguishing one garden from another since the tea is so strong.

Darjeeling. These are the rarest and most prestigious of black teas. They are generally sold in the best grade of whole leaves—G.F.O.P., T.G.F.O.P., and F.T.G.F.O.P. Highly esteemed gardens include Castleton, Bloomfield, Margaret's Hope, Namring and Gielle. Although it is rather difficult to distinguish one garden from another, the special flavor of each harvest period can be identified, for the taste of Darjeeling teas varies with the seasons. In general, these are afternoon teas taken plain, without milk (except when they are occasionally sold in broken-leaf form).

16- GRAND POUCHONG

17- TI KUAN YIN

18- TUNG TING

19- ASSAM T.G.F.O.P.

20- DARJEELING F.O.P.

First Flush Darjeeling. These are springtime teas, harvested from late February to mid-April. The young leaves yield a light tea with a flavor of green muscat. Their arrival is impatiently awaited by

An Indian tea merchant poses beside chests decorated with elegant calligraphy.

connoisseurs (not unlike the arrival of new Beaujolais wine), and they are sometimes specially air-freighted. A gentle, afternoon tea.

Second Flush Darjeeling. Harvested in May and June, these teas are more fully constructed than first flush varieties. The liquor is bright, the taste full and round with a fruity note. An afternoon tea.

In-Between Darjeeling. These intermediate teas are harvested in April and May, and combine the greenness of first flush teas with the maturity of second flush varieties.

Autumnal Darjeeling. These autumn-harvested Darjeelings are characterized by large leaves that give a round taste and coppery liquor. They can be drunk in the morning with a bit of cold milk.

Dooar. These are low-grown teas, dark and full-bodied, yet less strong than Assam teas. A daytime tea that goes well with a drop of milk.

Terai. Teas grown on the plain to the south of Darjeeling. The brew is richly colored, the taste spicy and liqueur-like. These teas can be drunk throughout the day and are often used in blends. They tolerate a bit of cold milk.

Travancore. Grown on the largest plantation in southern India, these teas produce a coppery liquor of strong, full-bodied flavor. They are intermediate teas that evoke teas from northern India while resembling Ceylon teas. A morning tea that may be taken with milk.

J a p a n

Japan produces only green tea. Low in theine yet unusually rich in vitamin C, these bracing and digestive teas are suitable beverages during and after meals. Yet they are also appropriate for a relaxing break. To be savored as is, without milk or sugar.

Genmaicha ("Japanese Rice"). A typically Japanese specialty—this medium-quality green tea is mixed with toasted rice and popped corn. To be sampled, out of curiosity, in the afternoon.

Gyokuro ("Precious Dew"). The flat, very green leaves of this tea are sharply pointed like pine needles and easily recognizable. This is the most refined of Japan teas—its liquor is greenish and its smooth taste remains long in the mouth. Given its cost, it is a tea to be drunk on special occasions.

Hojicha. A green tea that is roasted, producing brownish

21 - DOOARS T. G. F. O. P.

22 - TERAI T. G. F. O. P.

23 - TRAVANCORE F. B. O. P.

24 - GENMAICHA

25 - GYOKURO

leaves and liquor. Very light and low in theine, it pleasantly accompanies a meal.

Matcha Uji ("Froth of Liquid Jade"). Powdered tea made from Gyokuro leaves (although other, more common Matchas are made from less renowned leaves). In this specific case, Matcha Uji yields a jade green beverage that is concentrated and nourishing. It is perfect for making iced tea, as well as for coloring and flavoring sauces and sherbets.

Sencha Honyama. Like Gyokuro, this is one of Japan's great teas. It should be noted, however, that many types of Sencha exist, though few of them as prestigious as this one, with its pale green liquor, its fresh and flowery taste. A relaxing, afternoon tea.

TEA THE WORLD OVER

Starting in the nineteenth century, tea plantations spread across Asia and beyond, and began to be cultivated in regions of Africa, South America, the former Soviet Union, and the Near East. Production methods in these areas merit improvement,

A branch from a tea bush in flower, described in 1735 by J. B. Du Halde: "The flower is white, and has the form of a five-petaled rose. When the flowering season has passed, the plant produces berries that resemble a fleshy nut."

The Kuzmichev company has recently begun re-using the fine labels that adorned its containers of tea in the early 1900s. Gold dust is no longer used to embellish the labels, however, as it was in the days when Kuzmichev was purveyor to the top echelons of Saint Petersburg society.

for quantity is often placed above quality, as demonstrated by the mechanical harvesting techniques employed in the republic of Georgia. It must nevertheless be recognized that some "new" planters are now able to produce tea that rivals the finest varieties from India and Ceylon. It would therefore be a shame to deny oneself the pleasure of discovering them. At the English court, moreover, it is said that Her Majesty has become a fan of Cameroon tea—and it would hardly be proper to be more chauvinistic than the queen.

It should be noted that all the teas listed below are black teas; the cultivation and production of delicate green and semifermented teas remain the prerogative of countries possessing traditional, well-tested techniques.

ARGENTINA. Of medium body, tasting slightly of the local soil, these teas produce a dark liquor. They make an excellent morning tea and can be taken with a little cold milk.

BANGLADESH. The liquor is dark, the taste aromatic and slightly spicy. These are daytime teas, drunk with or without milk.

CAMEROON. High-quality, high-grown teas yielding a richly colored brew with an aromatic, malted taste. They can take a drop of cold milk and the broken-leaf grades in particular are perfect for the morning.

C.I.S. Russian tea is often

26 - HOJICHA

27 - MATCHA UJI

28 - SENCHA HONYAMA

29 - BANGLADESH G.F.O.P.

30 - CAMEROON F.B.O.P.

confused with "Imperial Russian" flavor, the latter being a blend of India and China teas flavored with citrus scents. "Real" Russian teas are generally grown in Georgia and are noted for their dark liquor, fairly full body and flowery taste. The whole-leaf grades produce decent afternoon or evening teas; the broken-leaf varieties are more appropriate in the morning, and can take a drop of cold milk.

MAURITIUS. These teas are characterized by their vanilla aroma. They are quite strong, go well with a little milk, and make a fine early-morning cup of tea.

INDONESIA. These teas are similar to those produced in Ceylon, for they are flavorful, fairly full and of a fine amber color. Perfect for the morning, particularly the broken-leaf grades. A little cold milk may be added to them.

IRAN. This tea makes a red brew that has all the lightness and mellowness of China teas. These afternoon teas are to be drunk plain.

KENYA. High-quality, Assam-like teas. Their liquor is golden, their flavor full and fruity. Perfect for the morning, with a drop of cold milk.

MALAYSIA. These broken-leaf teas produce a strong and forthright beverage appropriate for the morning, and can be taken with milk if desired.

NEPAL. The bright liquor of these teas, plus their fine, subtle and slightly fruity flavor,

A dried bouquet of green tea leaves bound together can be steeped directly in the cup, reviving the aroma and appearance of the fresh bouquet.

recall Darjeeling teas. To be taken plain, in the afternoon.

SIKKIM. High-quality teas grown on the high plateau of the Himalayas. Comparable to Darjeeling (to which they are geographically close), Sikkim teas nevertheless have more body and a hint of ripe fruit. The Temi gardens produce excellent Sikkim tea. An afternoon tea, to be appreciated as is.

TURKEY. The very mild, slightly sugary flavor of these teas recalls those of China. They come in whole-leaf grades to be drunk plain, in the evening.

CLASSIC BLENDS

Just as every wine owes its originality to a cellar master able to perfectly combine the qualities of various types of wine, so a tea taster must possess great skill in the art of blending. Tea tasters in the employ of major international retailers combine teas of various qualities to obtain a standardized product of predictable taste at a fixed price. These constitute the more "common" blends. Sometimes tea tasters act just like the "noses" of sophisticated perfume firms, inventing new blends that produce new aromas and thoroughly original tastes. This is done, for instance, by blending several great gardens from the same region to obtain a perfect

Didier Jumeau-Lafond, one of France's most knowledgeable tea experts.

31 - INDONESIA T.G.F.O.P.

32 - KENYA G.F.O.P.

33 - NEPAL G.F.O.P.

34 - SIKKIM T.G.F.O.P.

35 - TURKEY B.O.P.

balance of taste and color. Better still, the finest firms, by combining different types of tea from India to China, mixing black tea with green and fusing full-bodied and mild flavors, manage to produce teas whose origin cannot be pinpointed. This subtle alchemy makes every cup a delightful surprise.

The so-called "classic" blends that skillfully marry the aromas of various teas are the most difficult to produce—they are more subtle than the scented blends that simply sprinkle natural essences of flowers, leaves or fruit over the tea. With a little experience, however, a connoisseur can attempt a classic blend. There is no real recipe—a good scale, a healthy dose of intuition, and a few basic guidelines are all that are required. First of all, there is no point in blending teas with great character, for they will simply harm one another. Start with a neutral base, such as a China tea like Keemun, a South India tea (Nilgiri, Dooars, etc.), or even an African tea. These do not have an overwhelming personality yet will give the liquor a fine color. Then subtle notes may be added to this base—a little Lapsang Souchong for its smoky taste, or a hint of Darjeeling for its fruitiness, or even several grams of green tea to freshen and lighten the drink. Above all, however, it is important to know for what type of occasion and at what time of day the tea is to be served. As an example, the composition of two different types of classic blend are given below.

English Breakfast. A small-leaved tea generally composed of a Ceylon Broken Orange Pekoe with a hint of Assam or Darjeeling, or even another tea from South India or Africa. This very British blend is obviously drunk with a drop of milk and goes well with toast, honey and jam. It is not only ideal for breakfast, but can be enjoyed throughout the morning.

Five O'clock Tea. Another typically English blend, this time using whole-leaf Ceylon teas (O.P., F.O.P.). Somewhat full-bodied, the blend nevertheless gives a light, aromatic brew. Milk can be added, but the tea is delightful as is. An afternoon tea to be drunk on its own or with a snack of cakes and sweets.

SCENTED TEAS

The infatuation with scented teas that swept across France, Germany and Switzerland in the 1970s produced a veritable explosion of diverse—and sometimes bizarre—flavors that made purists shudder. So much so that it was often forgotten that this motley tribe of rhubarb, pistachio, coconut and chocolate teas descends from extremely refined Asian ancestors. Scented teas include a number of classics that are a delight to drink in the evening. Sugar may sometimes enhance their flavor, but milk is to be avoided.

Earl Grey. A China or Darjee-

36 · RUSSIAN O. P.

37 · FIVE O'CLOCK TEA

38 · EARL GREY

39 · JASMINE TEA

40 · ROSE TEA

ling tea (though green and semifermented teas are now sometimes used) scented with oil from the peel of bergamot, a Canton orange. Made fashionable by Earl Grey, the British prime minister, after a visit to China in 1830.

Jasmine or Rose Tea. The finest teas of this type come from China and are produced on the plantation itself, according to ancestral recipes. Freshly cut flowers are added to the tea so that it is impregnated with their aroma. Whether the flowers are subsequently removed or left in the tea makes little difference to the ultimate taste of the beverage, but nothing is more delightful than to find a few petals among the tea leaves.

Imperial Russian. Originally from China, but particularly appreciated by Russian high society in the nineteenth century, this tea is flavored with bergamot and other citrus scents.

Tea tasting was done in collaboration with Mariage Frères tea dealers in Paris.

TEA FOR GOURMETS

Westerners do not yet associate tea with gastronomy. People who frequent Chinese restaurants, of course, are used to the idea of savoring jasmine tea with exotic dishes. But such occasions provide only a faint glimmer of the infinite possibilities offered by tea. For it is entirely feasible to drink tea throughout a well-prepared Western-style meal, selecting the right tea with each course just as one would normally choose wines. Green or smoky tea goes well with fish, whereas Earl Grey, Darjeeling and Oolong are more appropriate with fowl. As to desserts, all the light, scented, large-leafed teas provide interesting options. There are, in fact, no precise rules—an adventurous palate and a little imagination are all that are required.

Furthermore, tea can be a delightful ingredient in gourmet recipes. The number of these recipes is limited because the subtle character of tea is easily overwhelmed by other, stronger flavors. Included below are nevertheless several delicate and refined combinations that are well worth trying.

Earl Grey Sauce

Ingredients: 1 cup chicken stock (bouillon cubes can be used), 1 heaping tablespoon Earl Grey tea, 1/4 cup heavy cream, 2 teaspoons of sugar, several drops of lemon juice, salt and pepper.
Bring the chicken stock to a boil, then steep the tea in it for three minutes. Boil cream with sugar over high heat until reduced by half. Strain stock and add to cream.
Reduce heat to low and continue to reduce, beating vigorously to produce a frothy texture. Add lemon juice and season with salt and pepper to taste. This sauce delightfully accompanies fowl, notably duck.

Matcha Sauce

Ingredients: 2 cups fish stock, 1/4 cup heavy cream, 1/4 teaspoon powdered Matcha or green Japan tea (do not exceed this amount, as the taste is very strong), several drops of lemon juice, salt and pepper.
Boil stock over high heat until reduced by half. Add cream and continue boiling until thick enough to coat the back of a spoon. Reduce heat to low, add Matcha and lemon juice and beat until a thick, light sauce is obtained. Season to taste with salt and pepper. Matcha sauce is delicious with sea trout and salmon.

Tea Jelly

Ingredients: 1 quart of steeped tea, 6 to 8 cups sugar, 1/2 cup apple pectin, juice of 1 1/2 lemons.
Bring the tea to a boil. Add the sugar, pectin and lemon juice. Bring back to a boil and continue cooking for four minutes. Place in jars, cover with a piece of plastic wrap and let cool.

Black Tea Ice Cream

Ingredients for four servings: 1/2 liter of milk, 5 egg yolks, 1 1/4 cups sugar, 1 tablespoon tea from Uva Highlands (a famous Ceylon tea estate).
Bring half the milk to a boil. Meanwhile, add the sugar to the egg yolks, beating until the mixture becomes whitish. Add it little by little to the cold milk and set aside. Steep the tea in the hot milk for four minutes, strain the leaves, and beat the hot milk into the egg yolk mixture. Pour into a pan and cook over very low heat for five minutes, stirring continuously with a wooden spoon. Cool completely and freeze according to manufacturer's instructions in an ice cream maker.

Tea Granita

Ingredients for eight servings: 1 cup Ceylon Orange Pekoe tea, 1 1/2 cups sugar, 2 tablespoons powdered milk, 1/4 cup white rum.
Steep the tea in 1 quart of boiling water for ten minutes. Strain the leaves and add 1 cup

This "Still-life with Tea" was photographed in the Mariage Frères tea salon. The foreground contains Mont Fuji, a creamy mousse made from green Japan tea, behind which can be seen a measure of powdered green Matcha Uji (in a spoon made from the bark of a cherry tree), a bowl of frothy tea, and the bamboo whisk used to whip the tea. On the left is a custard cream made with black tea, a bowl of tea jelly, a tea-scented candle, and a braid of tea to be plunged into a bathtub to perfume the water. The document concerns a shipment of tea imported by Mariage Frères in 1888.

of the sugar to the tea, stirring well. Pour into a glass or ceramic baking dish and place in the freezer.

When small patches of ice crystals appear on the surface, remove the dish from the freezer and transfer contents to a food processor. Add the powdered milk and process briefly to break up crystals. Return mixture to the freezer for ten minutes, then blend again. Repeat the operation about ten times until the mixture begins to resemble a cream. Add the rum and the remaining sugar. Blend one last time, return to the freezer briefly and serve immediately in individual bowls.

Green Tea Ice Cream

Ingredients for eight servings: 1 quart heavy cream, 2 cups milk, 1 1/4 cups sugar, a pinch of salt and 1/4 teaspoon green tea (preferably Matcha Uji).
Boil cream over high heat until reduced by half. Bring to room temperature, cover and refrigerate until well chilled.
Combine reduced cream with remaining ingredients and mix until sugar is dissolved. Pour into ice trays.

Mount Fuji

Ingredients for six servings: 1 cup milk, 1/2 cup powdered sugar, 6 egg yolks, 1 envelope gelatin, 1 scant teaspoon Matcha or green Japan tea, and 1 cup heavy cream.
Make a custard by blending the egg yolks and sugar until whitish. Heat the milk and the egg mixture, cooking over low heat and stirring continuously with a wooden spoon.
Sprinkle the gelatin over 1/4 cup cold water and let sit for five minutes to dissolve. When custard is creamy, take it off the heat and add the Matcha and the gelatin. It is important to let the mixture cool completely. Whip the cream and gently fold it into the cold custard.

Spoon into individual cups and place in the refrigerator for twenty-four hours.

Iced Tea

Iced tea is an outstandingly refreshing and invigorating drink, but should not be steeped in hot water, for it becomes cloudy and unattractive as it cools. Exceptionally clear iced tea can be obtained by steeping the tea in cold water and leaving it in the refrigerator for twelve hours.
The tea can then be drunk straight or on ice, or mixed with other ingredients to make cocktails.

Sakura Cocktail

Ingredients: Champagne, a simple sugar syrup made of equal amounts of sugar and water heated to dissolve then completely chilled, maraschino cherries and Sakura tea (12 cups tea for 1 quart of water).
Steep the tea in cold water. Add sugar syrup to taste. Chill champagne glasses, place a cherry in the bottom, then add 1/3 tea and 2/3 champagne.
Serve ice-cold.

Tea-Clipper Cocktail

Ingredients: Fresh apple juice, cinnamon tea (1/2 cup for 2 cups water), ice cubes.
Prepare cinnamon-flavored iced tea. Chill tall cocktail glasses. To serve, place ice cubes in the bottom of each glass and pour in 1/3 tea and 2/3 apple juice. Decorate with a slice of lime and serve ice cold.

The above recipes were provided by Mariage Frères, Paris, except for the Tea Granita and the iced tea drinks.

A CONNOISSEUR'S GUIDE

French author Jean-Paul Aron, in a preface to a book on chocolate, claimed that "tea evokes the calm of bedrooms, the warmth of Russian isbas, the reserve of English gentlemen. . . . The island-dwelling British are not the only Europeans to be keen on tea, for continentals consigned to wintry conviviality also appreciate it."

Excellent tea is now served on both sides of the English Channel, and the affirmation by Charles Laughton in Leo McCarey's 1935 film *Ruggles of Red Gap* that tea is "an English affair" is now something of a cliché. For it has also become "an international affair," as this guide to fine establishments in the United States, London and Paris shows, demonstrating that it is becoming easier to taste and buy high-quality tea and tea accessories.

TEA ROOMS

Below is a selection of the many tea rooms, or "tea salons," dotting the United States, London and Paris. Those listed have been selected because they offer an interesting range of standard and rare teas in a special setting.

NEW YORK

THE ALGONQUIN
59 West 44th Street (between 5th and 6th Avenues).
Famous for its literary days of the Round Table, this charming hotel in the middle of the theater district offers a wide array of teas. Pastries, English muffins, cinnamon toast, scones with Devonshire clotted cream as well as savory items like cheese with crackers and finger sandwiches are available every afternoon from 4:00 to 5:00.

THE BOOK FRIEND CAFÉ
16 West 18th Street (between 5th and 6th Avenues).
Actually a bookshop, this informal setting provides a comfortable place to browse while sipping tea selected from an interesting and varied menu. Tea sandwiches, scones and cakes are offered every afternoon from 3:00 to 5:00. The bookshop carries several good books devoted to tea and tea consumption.

MARK'S
The Mark Hotel, 25 East 77th Street (at Madison Avenue).
High tea is served daily in this elegant Upper East Side gem of a restaurant. Flawless service and excellent pastries make this a "must-do" for tea aficionados.

THE PALM COURT
The Plaza Hotel, 768 Fifth Avenue (at 58th Street).
People come from all over the country to enjoy the elegant English tea at the Plaza. From 3:45 to 6:00 Monday through Saturday (4:00 to 6:00 on Sunday), tea lovers can choose from fifteen varieties as well as scones, tiny sandwiches, miniature pastries and a full à la carte menu. Tea in this most regal of settings comes complete with chamber music and excellent service.

THE ROTUNDA
The Hotel Pierre, 795 Fifth Avenue (at 61st Street).
Tea is served in the beautiful Rotunda, an oval room with walls displaying a handsome mural. Elegant surroundings and impeccable service make the Pierre one of the best places in town to sample a carefully selected choice of fine teas as well as thin sandwiches, sumptuous pastries and scones.

THE STANHOPE
995 Fifth Avenue (at 81st Street).
Traditional tea is served every afternoon in the comfortable, intimate surroundings of this charming hotel, which is located right across the street from the Metropolitan Museum.

CHICAGO

THE CONSERVATORY
Chicago Four Seasons Hotel,
120 East Delaware
(Delaware and Michigan).
Located in the 900 North Michigan Building, the Conservatory is in the lounge area of the seventh-floor lobby overlooking Michigan Avenue. Monday through Friday, a full tea and a light tea are available from 3:00 to 5:00; Saturday from 3:30 to 5:00. A selection of loose-leaf teas is served along with pastries and scones. A piano player is a popular feature here.

THE PALM COURT

The Drake Hotel,
140 East Walton Place.

A seventeenth-century bronze urn and a beautiful fountain make a wonderful setting for a traditional afternoon tea. This historical landmark has become a Chicago institution, dating back to the 1920s. Comfortable sofas, lush green plants and dark paneling provide a re-

laxing, warm atmosphere for enjoying specialties like currant buns, scones and muffins served with whipped cream and homemade strawberry preserves. A harpist provides music every afternoon from 3:00 to 5:30.

LA TOUR

Park Hyatt Hotel, 800 North Michigan Avenue (at Chicago Avenue).

A three-tiered tea service with linen and fine china is served every day from 2:30 to 5:00. Tea is served in the Salon, located in the lounge area of the hotel. Pastries, sandwiches and scones are served with a basic selection of teas.

SAN FRANCISCO

CAMPTON PLACE

Campton Place Hotel, 340 Stockton Street (near Union Square).

The cozy lounge area serves tea daily from 2:30 to 4:30. Individual pots of tea are served in beautiful silver sets with a choice of pastries and sandwiches. A balanced selection of imported teas are all first-rate. Comfortable chairs and a suitable low-key setting make Campton Place the perfect place for sipping and chatting.

LOS ANGELES

RENDEZVOUS COURT

The Biltmore Hotel,
506 Grand Avenue.

Located in the hotel's former lobby, the cathedral-like, Spanish-Italian design provides a regal yet comfortable stage for tea. Stone columns, a carved two-story vaulted ceiling and a magnificent ornamental staircase combine to create a restful oasis after a busy day in Los Angeles. The Biltmore features a line of fine loose-leaf and herbal teas. A simple Rendezvous Tea entails a pot of tea and almond cookies. For the Traditional Tea, a tiered silver tea caddy is presented to the table fully laden with canapés, sandwiches and pastries.

WASHINGTON D.C.

THE FIREPLACE

The Jefferson Hotel,
1200 16th Street N.W.
(at M Street).

Afternoon tea here is quiet and quaint. The library-like setting is peaceful and soul-soothing, as is the constant glow of the fire. Traditional service includes cookies and fresh strawberries, smoked duck finger sandwiches and an array of teas from all corners of the world.

BOSTON

TEA COURT

Boston's Copely Plaza Hotel,
138 Saint James Avenue.

Located in the lobby of Boston's most stately hotel, the Tea Court is set back from the hustle and bustle, providing an agreeable sense of intimacy. Sofas, large chairs and small round tables make this a popular spot for conducting business or enjoying a quiet moment in pleasant surroundings. A full array of black and herbal teas is served along with sandwiches, pastries, cakes and scones. The date-nut bread is a popular choice among regulars.

LONDON

BROWN'S HOTEL

Albemarle Street, London W1.

Located just two minutes away from Hyde Park, Brown's is well known for its afternoon tea. Since tables cannot be reserved, customers begin lining up at three o'clock to make sure of obtaining one of the flowery chintz armchairs in the dark-paneled salon. Popular varieties include Darjeeling, Keemun, Gunpowder and Brown's Blend, acompanied by clotted cream, sandwiches, toast or cakes.

CLARIDGE'S

Brook Street,
Mayfair, London W1.

Tea can be taken in the "Reading Room," whose 1925 decor alone is worth the visit. Reservations are recommended.

MAIDS OF HONOUR

Newens 288 Kew Road,
Kew Gardens, Richmond, Surrey.

One of the oldest tea rooms in Great Britain, and therefore a must for all tea lovers and historians.

MAISON SAGNE

105 Marylebone High Street,
London W1.

A tea and pastry shop with a 1920s Pompeian decor right in the heart of the Marylebone district. The somewhat continental-style tea is served with excellent strawberry pies, walnut, chocolate or praline pastries, croissants or buns.

RITZ HOTEL

Piccadilly, London W1.

Tea is served in the Palm Court's superb nineteenth-century setting. The elegance of Ritz service is notorious, thanks to the variety of finger sandwiches made of cucumber, salmon, turkey, etc. Scones are accompanied by strawberry jam and clotted cream. Reservations are required if one is not staying at the hotel.

SAVOY HOTEL

The Strand, London WC2.

Tea at the Savoy is a grand London tradition. The well-trained and friendly staff place teapots and cakes on rattan tables in a room decorated with a trompe l'oeil fresco, overlooking the Thames.

WALDORF HOTEL

Aldwych, London WC2.

The British tradition of tea dances is still alive in the indoor garden of the Palm Court Lounge with its palm trees and orchestra. Between two waltzes, dancers enjoy Earl Grey, Darjeeling, Lapsang Souchong or a special blend accompanied by cakes and sandwiches.

TEA TIME

21 The Pavement
Clapham, London SW4.

This fashionable tea room was founded by Jane Pettigrew, author of *Tea Time*. The many varieties of tea are accompanied by cakes and pastries made following the original recipes found in Pettigrew's book.

PARIS

ANGELINA

1) 226 Rue de Rivoli
75001 Paris.
2) Palais des Congrès (Level 3)
24 Blvd. Pershing
75017 Paris.
3) Galeries Lafayette Department Store (Third Floor)
27 Rue de la Chaussée-d'Antin
75008 Paris.

The original salon on the Rue de Rivoli has now been listed as being of historical interest, and the tea (in-

---

JAPANESE TEA CEREMONY

Visitors to Paris wishing to learn about the Japanese tea ceremony may contact the Urasenke Foundation, 142 Boulevard Masséna (Apt. 12.11), 75013 Paris. Alternatively, one can reserve a place in the traditional pavilion built in the Albert-Kahn gardens in Boulogne, where tea is served every Tuesday and Sunday morning (Tel. 46 04 52 80).

---

cluding Darjeeling and Lapsang Souchong) is served in silver teapots. The Darjeeling is particularly special because it is cultivated in Angelina's own "garden." Patrons may also buy Angelina's eleven varieties of tea in the adjoining shop.

À PRIORI THÉ

35-37, Galerie Vivienne
75002 Paris.

In a large, quiet room decorated in tones of beige, under a skylight, habi-

tués of A Priori Thé sample one of the tea room's sixteen classic or scented blends. This is one of the few Paris salons to offer mint tea.

L'ARBRE À CANNELLE

57 Passage des Panoramas
75002 Paris.

The fine peristyle on L'Arbre à Cannelle's Napoleon III façade attracts both the curious and connoisseurs. The recently restored setting is the perfect place to have breakfast or a simple cup of tea. Fifteen teas are offered, each clearly decribed on the menu. For afternoon tea, the Makaibari from Darjeeling or an excellent Ceylon is recommended.

LA COUR DE ROHAN

59-61 Rue Saint-André-des-Arts
75005 Paris.

Known for its elegant and luxurious charm, this plush salon teas offers

eighteen teas, one of which is a Cour de Rohan blend produced by the owner himself. All teas are served in antique porcelain, and on Saturday nights the tea room is open late.

LADURÉE

16 Rue Royale
75008 Paris.

This attractive tea room with its painted ceilings typical of the nineteenth century is known for its macaroons that go delightfully well with one of the three straightforward teas from Betjeman and Barton.

LES ENFANTS GÂTÉS

43 Rue des Francs-Bourgeois
75004 Paris.

This combination art gallery and English club makes for a comfortable atmosphere. The menu provides clear and interesting explanations. A high-grown Darjeeling, a Keemun or an imaginatively scented tea is perfect for a delightful brunch or afternoon tea break.

INTERCONTINENTAL HOTEL

3 Rue de Castiglione
75001 Paris.

Real English tea can be had in the Lobby Bar—to the strains of a harp—or on the terrace. A good selection of seven teas is served in Wedgwood china, accompanied by English muffins, scones, cakes, cucumber sandwiches and even Devonshire clotted cream. Not a single detail has been overlooked.

LE LOIR DANS LA THÉIERE

3 Rue des Rosiers
75004 Paris.

Settle into an armchair or sofa and while away the time over a cup of one of the thirty-seven teas on the menu (including many scented varieties), admiring the old cupboards and a fresco of Alice in Wonderland decorating the salon.

MAISON BLANCHE 15 MONTAIGNE

15 Avenue Montaigne
75008 Paris.

Have tea in one of the most spectacular settings in Paris: the rooftop restaurant on the Théâtre des

Champs-Elysées (the terrace is open in summer). A choice of eleven rare teas, including green Sencha Ariake tea from Japan and red Bourbon tea from Africa (theine-free). Served with scones and English muffins.

MARIAGE FRÈRES

1) 30-32 Rue du Bourg-Tibourg
75004 Paris.
2) 13, Rue des Grands-Augustins
75006 Paris.

Tea rooms have been opened alongside the age-old tea counters at each of the famous Mariage outlets. The skylit Bourg-Tibourg salon evokes the warm colonial climate and, behind the bar, a specialist prepares and tastes each tea. If you don't know what to order, one of the white-garbed waiters will skillfully guide you through the list of three hundred and fifty teas (plus special additions depending on availability).

This is the place to be seduced by a white tea from Fujian (for true connoisseurs only), by tea jellies, or by the trolley of delicious pies and tea-flavored desserts. Over on Rue des Grands Augustins, in a seventeenth-century residence officially listed as a historical site, tea is taken either in a vaulted cellar evoking the "tea docks" from colonial days, or on an upper floor bedecked with tall, elegant windows. Sunday brunch is highly fashionable at both establishments.

LE MEURICE

228 Rue de Rivoli
75001 Paris.

In the very fine setting of its Pompadour Salon, the Meurice Hotel offers fifteen varieties of tea, including classic and scented blends. All are served in silver teapots, accompanied by toast, cakes or petit fours.

MOSQUE

19 Rue Geoffroy-Saint-Hilaire
75005 Paris.

The Paris Mosque's café is the only place in town where traditional North African mint tea can be savored in a superbly Moorish interior (winter) or on a cool patio (summer).

LE PLAZA ATHENÉE

21 Avenue Montaigne
75008 Paris.

The hotel's Gobelins Gallery proposes a selection of four teas, to be savored to the sound of a piano. Meanwhile, the Relais Plaza restaurant (a reconstitution of the dining room on the cruise ship *Normandie*) offers a full English tea to the strains of a harp. Toasted buns, scones, tiny sandwiches and cream accompany one of twenty-three teas, including the Plaza's Secret Blend.

HOTEL RITZ

15 Place Vendôme
75001 Paris.

Every day at four o'clock, afternoon tea can be had at the Vendôme bar.

Sit back in a plush sofa in winter, or enjoy the fine terrace in summer. Twelve teas, including a good green tea and a theine-free variety, are served along with sandwiches, petit fours and hot muffins.

TEA CADDY

14 Rue Saint-Julien-le Pauvre
75005 Paris.

Located opposite a charming little church, this very British tea room has remained unchanged since it was founded in 1928 by a Miss Kinklin. The last generals of the Indian Army often met there to reminisce. Nostalgia comes in the form of a dozen teas, including Imperial Russian, Lapsang Souchong, Assam and Darjeeling, accompanied by delicious homemade cakes.

TORAYA

10 Rue Saint-Florentin,
75001 Paris.

Purveyors to His Majesty the Emperor of Japan for four hundred years, the Toraya firm has recently opened a salon in Paris decorated in black lacquer and bamboo. It offers two green teas—a Sencha and a Matcha—prepared strictly according to traditional rules and accompanied by a *zangetsu* or other sweet made from *adzuki* beans. Both teas are imported directly from Japan and are also sold in a shop next to the tea room.

TEA SHOPS

Where can you go to seek advice and buy tea, who knows the most about Russian or Japanese teas, and where can you find a broad selection of teapots? To answer these questions, several outstanding American and European merchants are given below.

NEW YORK

BLOOMINGDALES
100 Third Avenue (between 59th and 60th Streets).
Highly select teas are sold in the food department of this most famous of department stores. Exotic teas like Ceylonese Berubeul, Indian Travancore Highgrown and Japanese Sencha grace the shelves. Bloomingdales has just introduced the exclusive Mariage Frères teas from Paris, an American first.

MCNULTY'S TEA AND COFFEE COMPANY
109 Christopher Street (between Bleeker and Hudson).
A Greenwich Village institution, McNulty's offers some of the best teas available in New York. Earl Grey, English Breakfast and Darjeeling are among the favorites. Japan teas sold here are Bancha, Japan Green Pan-Fired brands, and China teas include Gunpowder, Young Hyson and Lung Ching. The toll-free number for mailing and shipping is: 800 356 5200.

PORTO RICO
201 Bleeker Street (between 6th and MacDougal Street).
People line up to buy teas from all over the world at this New York landmark. Darjeeling, Assam and an assortment of green teas are among the 100 varieties available. The toll-free order and shipping number is: 800 453 53 08.

LONDON

FORTNUM AND MASON
181 Piccadilly
London W1.
Fortnum and Mason is a veritable institution, having been suppliers to the British aristocracy for nearly three hundred years. The ever-popular tea department offers forty varieties in green or red tins, including Darjeeling, Assam, Ceylon, Formosa and China teas as well as the famous blends named Royal, Crown, Celebration, Breakfast, Fortmason, New York, Queen Anne, et cetera. Several Fortnum and Mason teas may also be sampled on the premises.

HARRODS
Knightsbridge, London SW1.
In the amazing setting of Harrod's famous "Food Hall," the tea department sells Betjeman and Barton teas. Prince Charles reportedly prefers the Pushkin blend with its aroma of bergamot and other citrus flavors.

TEA HOUSE
15a Neal Street
Covent Garden, London WC2.
This unusual shop with its red-and-black brick façade offers forty-five varieties of tea from India, China and Japan, as well as a full range of "Teaphernalia," tea-related products and utensils. Tea may be ordered by mail. Tea House outlets are also located in Oxford and Stratford-upon-Avon.

TWININGS
216 The Strand
London WC2.
Founded in 1706 by Thomas Twining, this is the oldest tea shop in London. It offers a selection of over fifty teas, and houses a small museum displaying the biggest teapot in the world.

WHITTARD & CO., LTD.
81 Fulham Road
Chelsea, London SW3.
One of London's oldest tea merchants, Whittard & Company import directly from China, Japan, Ceylon and Formosa. Their popular varieties include Mango Indica, Spice Imperial and first flush Darjeelings.

PARIS

BETJEMAN AND BARTON
a) 23 Boulevard Malesherbes
75008 Paris.
b) 24 Boulevard des Filles-du-Calvaire
75003 Paris.
This shop is regularly visited by tealovers. Every day, a cup of one of the hundred and twenty teas stored in either red or green canisters (and fully described in Betjeman and Barton's catalogue) is offered to customers—with any luck you may drop in when a Saint James Fannings or a Castleton G.F.O.P. second flush is being brewed. The store also sells teapots, strainers, infusers, whisks for Matcha, metallic and lac-

quer containers, and fine wooden tea caddies, not to mention B & B's exclusive nylon teabags that preserve the full flavor of the four teas thus packaged. Furthermore, customers will find scones, crumpets, English muffins, mince pies and tea jellies. The firm is headed by Didier Jumeau-Lafond, a renowned tea connoisseur. Betjeman and Barton was founded in Paris in 1919, and now exports to Japan, Australia, the United States, and elsewhere. For a modest fee you can purchase their well-produced catalogue known as "the little book of tea."

BRÛLERIE DE L'ODÉON
6 Rue Crébillon
75006 Paris.
This is the capital's oldest tea and coffee merchant. It also stocks the widest selection of Fortnum and Mason teas in Paris, offering over twenty blends such Royal Blend, Earl Blend, Jasmine, Orange Pekoe, Darjeeling, Breakfast and Fortmason in tin containers or teabags as well as in bulk. There are a few tables at which customers can sample a cup of tea.

COMPAGNIE ANGLAISE DES THÉS
1 Rue Pierre Lescot
75001 Paris.
Founded in 1823, and once official purveyor to Napoleon III, this tiny shop is just a stone's throw from the Champs-Elysées. The wood-paneled interior houses a hundred varieties of tea, including fine Darjeelings, a China Paklum, and the famous Lotus Flower Tea. One Darjeeling comes in muslin teabags, and the store sells a range of imaginative teapots. Personal blends can also be ordered. Other outlets have been opened on Rue Lecourbe and at the Forum des Halles.

LES CONTES DE THÉ
60 Rue du Cherche-Midi
75006 Paris.
In addition to a good selection of Ceylon, Assam, Darjeeling and China teas, this boutique stocks teas from Brazil and Mauritius. The eighty-five varieties also include an unusual green Japan Hojicha, a grilled tea of light and incomparable flavor, to be drunk with meals. A wide range of scented teas from England are sold in teabag form. Three hundred and fifty teapots, many of eccentric design, are also on sale along with tea caddies, samovars and tea cozies.

L'ÉPICERIE
51 Rue Saint-Louis-en-l'Isle
75004 Paris.
This old-fashioned-looking épicerie, or dry-goods store, lined with characteristic wood paneling and shelves laden with honey, jams and other treats, offers an excellent selection of classic black teas sold in bulk and in attractive blue metal containers. The shop also boasts five exclusive blends that are rather "British" in nature and therefore perfect for breakfast or brunch.

ESTRELLA
34 Rue Saint-Sulpice
75006 Paris.
This little shop sells one hundred and twenty teas in bulk, a number of which also come in 125 gram (3 1/2 oz.) packets. Estrella creates its own aromatic blends and stocks a dozen different Darjeelings, as well as a se-

lection of teas from Fortnum and Mason and Jackson's of Piccadilly.

FAUCHON
28 Place de la Madeleine
75008 Paris.
This prestigious Paris catering firm was founded over a century ago, and includes a tea department that sells sixty varieties of tea in bulk, including excellent high-grown harvests, exclusive blends, and scented teas. Fans of Darjeeling will appreciate the Jungpana, with its delicious aroma of ripe peaches, or may sample the Kee-Yu, an unusual and especially smooth blend of China teas. Every day a different cup of tea is offered to customers for tasting.

GALERIES LAFAYETTE
40 Boulevard Haussmann
75009 Paris.
The "gourmet" boutique in this vast department store sells forty varieties of tea, notably a range of Asian teas, including six Darjeelings, a Formosa Gunpowder, and three green Japan teas as well as many scented teas. A cup of tea may be sampled at the counter.

HÉDIARD
21 Place de la Madeleine
75008 Paris.
In a small red shop just off the square, a knowledgeable saleswoman can suggest one of Hédiard's one hundred teas, including twenty-eight classic varieties, three theine-free teas, and seventy scented blends. The famous Hédiard Blend sits alongside a superb range of outstanding Darjeelings such as the ever-so-subtle Puttabong. Hédiard also carries a selection of teabags, packaged mint tea (mint and sugar already added), and a few Fortnum and Mason blends.

MARIAGE FRÈRES
a) 30-32 Rue du Bourg-Tibourg
75004 Paris.
b) 13 Rue des Grands-Augustins
75006 Paris.
On entering either of these enticing shops, customers feel as though they have walked onto a movie set or back into the past. Near a colonial-style counter, between chests of tea from China, are displayed canisters of over three hundred and fifty types of tea. The tricky task of choosing one is facilitated by the purchase of a small catalogue and by the competent sales staff who can guide you through the thirty tea-producing countries, the exclusive blends and the amazing Darjeelings such as Puttabong and Upper Namring. Over three hundred tea services, old and new, are sold alongside samovars, infusers, rock sugar, containers in metal or cherry bark, and even tea-scented candles. There are also four types of jelly and sweets made from tea and five varieties of chocolate with tea-flavored fillings. There are even braided mats of tea to be plunged into the bathtub to perfume the water. There is obviously a wide range of teapots on sale, whether cast-iron, porcelain, ceramic, or silver-plated (including the 1930 model used in the tea room, which keeps the tea at the right temperature). Finally, customers may wish to buy a reproduction of a seventeenth-century English tea caddy made of precious

wood. Mariage Frères has recently opened a Tea Museum in the Rue du Bourg-Tibourg outlet, where rare objects from the eighteenth and nineteenth century are displayed.

MARKS AND SPENCER

35 Boulevard Haussmann
75009 Paris.

This English department store distributes a dozen classic types of tea under its own brand name, St. Michael. Earl Grey, Darjeeling, Extra Strong, Breakfast, Fine Flavor and other blends are also available. Marks and Spencer in Paris and in the French provinces also stocks buns, scones and English muffins—all the ingredients for an authentic English afternoon tea.

LE PALAIS DES THÉS

a) 35 Rue de l'Abbé-Grégoire
75006 Paris.
b) 21 Rue Raymond-Losserand
75014 Paris.

Three hundred types of tea are displayed in canisters, each one listed in the "tea-lover's handbook." The shop also sells old and new samovars, teapots, and all the utensils needed for the tea ritual. There is also a complete tea-lover's library that shows a marked penchant for Russian teas. You can try out your samovar with teas from Georgia, Azerbaijan, and the Caucasus, as well as nine Russian Imperial blends. Le Palais des Thés also proposes its famous Monks' Tea and the Compagnie Coloniale brand of muslin teabags. The store accepts mail orders.

TWININGS

76 Boulevard Haussmann
75008 Paris.

In this very British shop one can find the full range of teas from Twinings, official purveyors to the British royal family. Tea is generally sold in 200 gram (5 1/2 oz.) tins or in teabags, but a selection is sold in bulk. There are sixty scented teas (whisky, cinnamon with bits of cinnamon stick, and others), thirty-three classic varieties, and such rarities as Persian tea. A wide selection of teapots is also available.

GLOSSARY

ASSAM: A region in northeastern India known for its strong, high-grade tea.

AUTUMNAL: India and Formosa teas harvested in autumn, and therefore touched with cool weather.

BASKET-FIRED: Japan tea that has been cured in baskets by firing.

BLACK TEA: Tea that has been withered, rolled (or macerated), fermented, fired (or dried), and sorted into grades.

BLENDER: A taster who decides on the proportions of each variety required to produce the flavor of a given blend.

BRICK TEA: Common grades of China and Japan teas mixed with stalk and dust and molded into bricks under high pressure.

BROKEN ORANGE PEKOE (B.O.P.): Black tea comprising smaller leaves and broken segments with some tips, harvested by the fine plucking method. When an abundance of tips is included, the grade becomes F.B.O.P. (Flowery Broken Orange Pekoe).

BROKEN PEKOE (B.P.): Full-bodied black tea comprising broken segments of somewhat coarse leaves, without tips.

CACHAR: The most common variety of India tea, produced in the Cachar district of Assam.

CAMELLIA SINENSIS: Botanical name for the tea plant.

CEYLON: Former name of Sri Lanka, still occasionally used when referring to tea grown on the island.

CHING WO: Black China tea from Fujian province.

CHUNMEE: Green China tea, so called due to its resemblance to the shape of human eyebrows.

CONGOU: A general term used to describe all black teas from China, irrespective of district.

C.T.C.: Crushing/Tearing/Curling. A mechanized method of macerating tea (as opposed to rolling) that speeds fermentation of black teas and accelerates production time.

DARJEELING: A province in northern India that produces black tea famous for its exquisite bouquet.

DIMBULA: A district in Sri Lanka (Ceylon) that produces full-bodied black tea.

DOOARS: A district in northern India that produces a black tea of the same name.

DUST: Black tea in small siftings of less than a millimeter, practically reduced to powder.

EARL GREY: A black China tea scented with oil of bergamot.

ENGLISH BREAKFAST: A name originally applied to China Congou in the United States, and now used to include blends of black teas in which the China flavor predominates.

ESTATE: A property or holding that may include more than one garden under the same management or ownership.

FANNINGS: Small grainy particles of leaf (1 to 1.5 millimeters) sifted out of the better-grade teas. They produce a liquor that is often as good as that of whole leaf grades.

FERMENTATION: A stage in the production of black tea involving oxidation of enzymes naturally found in the tea leaf.

FLOWERY ORANGE PEKOE: Orange Pekoe with an abundance of tips, and therefore of finer quality.

FLOWERY PEKOE: Whole-leaf black tea with the leaves rolled lengthwise.

FLUSH: Young tea leaf shoots. The term also refers to the various harvests—thus "first flush" is the early, spring plucking whereas "second flush" is harvested in late spring and early summer.

FORMOSA: The island known as Taiwan. Produces Oolong, Pouchong and black teas.

GARDEN: The name of a specific plantation, used to identify fine harvests produced solely from that garden. In Ceylon, gardens are sometimes referred to as "estates."

GOLDEN TIPS: Orange-colored buds found in certain black teas.

(Glossary continued on page 251)

STATISTICS ON
TEA

Tea is known the world over, but is not drunk everywhere to the same extent. Recent years have witnessed a general increase in consumption, notably on the Indian sub-continent. The Irish and the British, however, remain the champion tea-drinkers, even though their average consumption per head has stagnated or even slightly fallen.

French imports, on the other hand, have risen steadily since 1960, going from 1,647 metric tons to 6,326 metric tons in 1988. According to a Nielssen marketing survey, department stores and supermarkets account for 8% of total tea sales, 74% of which are sold in teabag form. French women drink twice as much tea as men, while young people are turning increasingly to the beverage thanks both to newer scented blends and to worldwide travel that introduces them to the social customs of other countries.

The latest statistics still indicate the former Soviet Union as the world's largest importer of tea, having bought 227,000 metric tons in 1989, just ahead of Great Britain with 200,000 tons.

The map shows in dark green the tea-producing regions of the following countries: Australia, Bangladesh, Bhutan, Burma, Burundi, China, India, Indonesia, Iran, Japan, Kenya, Korea, Malawi, Malaysia, Mauritius, Mozambique, Nepal, Rwanda, Sri Lanka, Taiwan, Tanzania, Thailand, Turkey, Uganda, ex-USSR, Vietnam, Zaire, and Zimbabwe.
A few countries not shown on the map also produce tea: Argentina, Brazil, Cameroon, Ecuador and Peru.

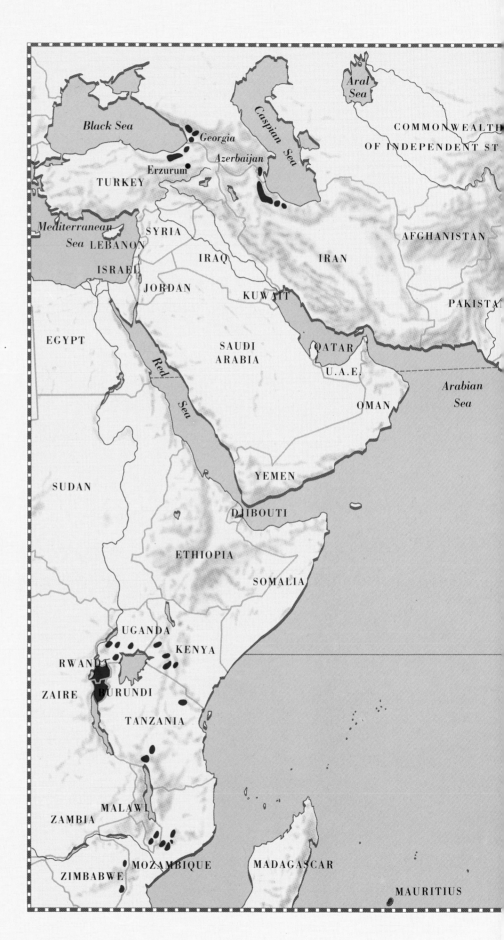

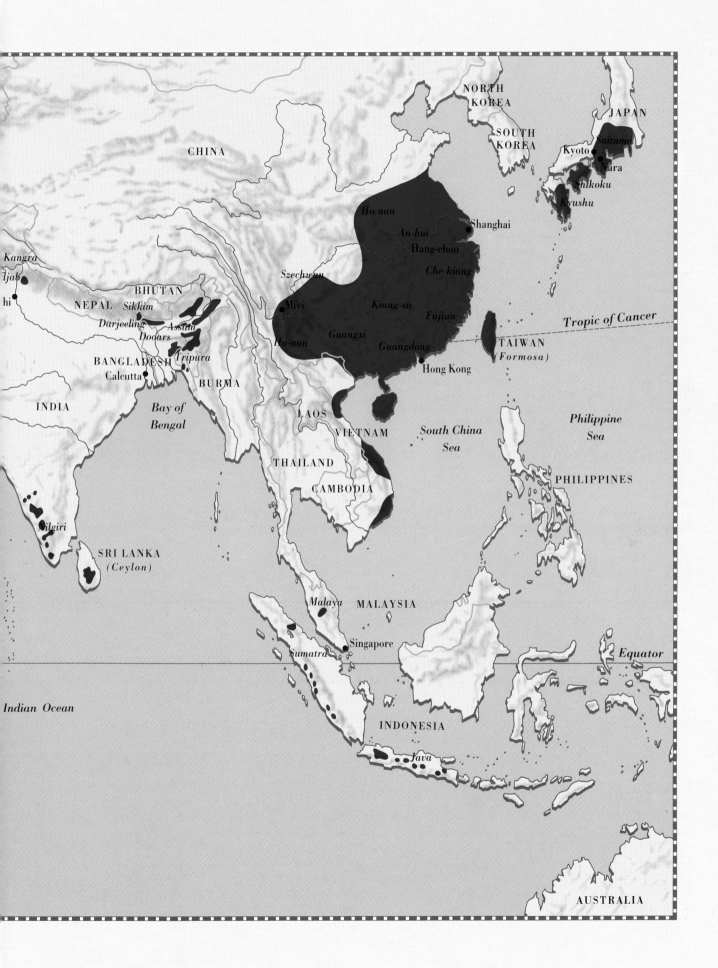

Worldwide production of tea remains high, with India, China and Sri Lanka (Ceylon) still supplying the lion's share. Serious efforts are now being made, however, by African countries (particularly Kenya, which accounts for 60% of all tea produced on the African continent).

Looking toward the year 2000, the World Bank forecasts significant increases in production by India (rising to 860,000 tons), Indonesia (157,000 tons) and Kenya (250,000 tons, bringing that country up to Sri Lankan levels).

The figures given here were supplied by the Comité Français du Thé (Suresnes, France) and the International Tea Committee (London, England).

AVERAGE ANNUAL CONSUMPTION PER HEAD 1988-1990	
Ireland	3.09 kg
United Kingdom	2.74 kg
Turkey	2.24 kg
Qatar	2.17 kg
Iraq	2.14 kg
Hong Kong	1.82 kg
Kuwait	1.62 kg
New Zealand	1.58 kg
Tunisia	1.47 kg
Egypt	1.38 kg
Bahrain	1.31 kg
Syria	1.25 kg
Sri Lanka	1.22 kg
Jordan	1.21 kg
Morocco	1.16 kg
Saudi Arabia	1.14 kg
Australia	1.07 kg
ex-USSR	1.04 kg
Japan	0.97 kg
Pakistan	0.95 kg
Chile	0.85 kg
Poland	0.84 kg
Kenya	0.71 kg
Netherlands	0.66 kg
India	0.59 kg
Canada	0.53 kg
Denmark	0.40 kg
USA	0.34 kg
Sweden	0.32 kg
Germany	0.21 kg
France	0.19 kg
China	not available

Note: 1 kg = approximately 500 cups

WORLD PRODUCTION OF TEA IN THOUSANDS OF METRIC TONS 1990	
India	715
China	540
Ceylon (Sri Lanka)	234
Kenya	197
Indonesia	150
Turkey	131
ex-USSR	110
Japan	90
Iran	55
Bangladesh	45
Vietnam	40
Malawi	39
Argentina	34
Formosa (Taiwan)	22
Tanzania	18
Zimbabwe	17
Rwanda	13
South Africa	12
Brazil	10
Papua New Guinea	8
Uganda	7
Mauritius	6
Malaysia	5
Burundi	4
Zaire	3
Peru	3
Cameroon	2
Ecuador	2
Mozambique	2
Australia	1

Approximately 2.5 million tons of tea were produced in 1990, of which green tea constituted roughly 0.6 tons

(Continued from page 247)

GOVERNMENT STANDARDS: Grades of teas selected annually as import standards of purity, quality and fitness for consumption by the U.S. Board of Tea Experts.

GREEN TEA: Unfermented tea that is immediately heated (or steamed) to kill the fermentation enzymes. Then it is rolled and dried.

GUNPOWDER: A type of young green tea, each leaf of which is rolled into a ball.

GYOKURO: Japanese for "pearl dew." A high-grade tea made by a special process in the Uji district of Japan, using tea grown on shaded bushes.

HIGH TEA: An afternoon or evening meal with meat and other dishes at which tea is the main beverage.

HYSON: Chinese for "flourishing spring." A type of green China tea, formerly drunk extensively in Europe. "Young Hyson" is a type of China tea plucked early.

KEEMUN (or KEEMUM): A fine grade of black-leaf China Congou tea produced in Anhui province.

KENYA: A country in Africa that produces one of the finest black teas from that continent.

LAPSANG SOUCHONG: A smoky China tea.

LEGG CUT: A mechanized method for cutting leaves prior to fermentation and firing. Eliminates the withering stage and produces Fannings and Dust grade teas.

MATCHA: Powdered green tea from Japan, used in the tea ceremony.

NATURAL LEAF: Whole-leaf green tea from Japan, similar to "pan-fired" but with less rolling, also known as "porcelain-fired."

NILGIRI: A district in the hills of southern India that produces black tea.

OOLONG: Semifermented tea from China or Formosa.

ORANGE PEKOE (O.P.): Black tea comprising leaves 8 to 15 millimeters long. It has fewer tips than F.O.P. because it is plucked somewhat later in the season.

PAN-FIRED: A kind of Japan tea that is steamed, then rolled in iron pans over charcoal fires.

PEKOE: A grade of black tea produced by a medium plucking of the second leaf on the bush.

PEKOE SOUCHONG: Black tea, each leaf of which is rolled in a ball, produced by a coarse plucking of the third leaf on the bush.

POUCHONG: A kind of scented China tea, so called from the Cantonese method of packing in small paper packets, each of which was supposed to be the produce of one choice tea plant.

ROLLING: A stage in manufacture designed to break down the cell walls of the tea leaf so that it releases its essential oils.

SCENTED TEA: Green, semifermented or black tea that has been flavored by the addition of flowers, fruit or essential oils. Earl Grey is one of the most famous of scented teas.

SEMIFERMENTED TEA: Tea that has been partially fermented, lending it qualities halfway between green tea and black tea.

SENCHA: The most popular variety of green tea in Japan.

SMOKY TEA: Black tea from China or Formosa that has been smoked over a wood fire.

SORTING: A stage in manufacturing in which the leaves are sifted, or sorted, into different sizes and grades.

SPRING TEAS: Formosa teas picked in the April-May season.

SUMMER TEAS: Formosa teas picked in the June-September season.

SZECHWAN: A non-smoky black tea from China, with narrow leaves and flowery fragrance.

TANNIN: An astringent chemical constituent of tea.

TARRY SOUCHONG: Very smoky black tea from China or Formosa.

TEA CADDY: A small container (often with lock and key) for tea, from *catty*, the Chinese and/or Malayan word for "pound," the quantity of tea originally contained in a caddy.

TEA TASTER: An expert judge of leaf and cup quality at all stages of production, brokerage, and final packaging.

THEINE: Another name for the caffeine contained in tea.

TIP: The bud leaf on a tea plant.

TIPPY TEAS: Teas with white or golden tips.

UVA: A district in Ceylon (Sri Lanka) that produces a tea of great subtlety.

WITHERING: The initial stage in the manufacture of black tea, designed to reduce moisture content in the leaves so that they can be rolled or macerated.

YUNNAN: Black tea from the Yunnan province of China. Along with Assam, this region was the original site of wild tea plants.

TEA TASTING GLOSSARY

Terms Describing Dry Leaf

BLACK: A black appearance is desirable, preferably with "bloom."

BLACKISH: A satisfactory appearance for CTC-type teas. Denotes careful sorting.

BLOOM: A sign of good manufacture and sorting (where the reduction of leaf has mainly taken place before firing), a "sheen" that has not been lost through over-handling or over-sorting.

BOLD: Particles of leaf which are too large for the particular grade.

BROWN: A brown appearance in CTC-type teas that normally indicates overly harsh treatment of the leaf.

CHESTY: Inferior or unseasoned packing materials create this taint.

CHUNKY: A very large broken-leaf tea.

CLEAN: Leaf that is free from fiber, dust and all extraneous matter.

CREPY: A crimped appearance common to larger-grade broken-leaf teas such as B.O.P.

CURLY: The leaf appearance of whole-leaf grade teas such as O.P., as distinct from "wiry."

EVEN: True to the grade, consisting of pieces of leaf of fairly even size.

FLAKY: Flat, open and often light in texture.

GRAY: Caused by too much abrasion during sorting.

GRAINY: Describes primary grades of well-made CTC teas such as Pekoe Dust.

LEAFY: A tea in which leaves tend to be on the large or long side.

LIGHT: A tea light in weight, of poor density. Sometimes flaky.

MAKE: Well-made tea (or not), true to its grade.

MUSHY: A tea that has been packed or stored with a high moisture content.

MUSTY: A tea affected by mildew.

NEAT: A grade having good "make" and size.

NOSE: Smell of the dry leaf.

POWDERY: Fine light dust.

RAGGED: An uneven, badly manufactured and graded tea.

STALK & FIBER: Should be minimal in superior grades, but is generally unavoidable in lower-grade teas.

TIP: A sign of fine plucking, apparent in top grades of tea.

UNEVEN & MIXED: "Uneven" pieces of leaf usually indicative of poor sorting and not true to the particular grade.

WELL TWISTED: Used for describing whole-leaf grades, often referred to as "well-made" or "rolled."

WIRY: Leaf appearance of a well-twisted, thin-leaf tea.

Terms Describing Infused Leaf

AROMA: Smell or scent denoting "inherent character," usually in tea grown at high altitudes.

BISCUITY: A pleasant aroma often found in a well-fired Assam.

BRIGHT: A lively bright appearance. Usually indicates bright liquors.

COPPERY: Bright leaf that indicates a well-manufactured tea.

DULL: Lacks brightness and usually denotes poor tea. Can be due to faulty manufacture and firing, or a high moisture content.

DARK: A dark or dull color that usually indicates poorer leaf.

GREEN: When referring to black tea, refers to underfermentation or to leaves from immature bushes (liquors often raw or light). Can also be caused by poor rolling.

MIXED OR UNEVEN: Leaf of varying color.

TARRY: A smoky aroma.

Terms Describing Liquors

BAGGY: A taint normally resulting from unlined hessian bags.

BAKEY: An over-fired liquor. Tea in which too much moisture has been driven off.

BODY: A liquor having both fullness and strength, as opposed to being thin.

BRASSY: Unpleasant metallic quality similar to brass. Usually associated with unwithered tea.

BRIGHT: Denotes a lively fresh tea with good keeping quality.

BRISK: The most "live" characteristic. Results from good manufacture.

BURNED: Extreme over-firing.

CHARACTER: An attractive taste, specific to origin, describing teas grown at high altitudes.

COARSE: Describes a harsh, undesirable liquor.

COLORY: Indicates useful depth of color and strength.

COMMON: A very plain, light and thin liquor with no distinct flavor.

CREAM: A precipitate obtained after cooling.

DRY: Indicates slight over-firing.

DULL: Not clear, and lacking any brightness or briskness.

EARTHY: Normally caused by damp storage, but can also describe a taste that is sometimes "climatically inherent" in teas from certain regions.

EMPTY: Describes a liquor lacking fullness. No substance.

FLAT: Not fresh (usually due to age).

FLAVOR: A most desirable extension of "character," caused by slow growth at high elevations. Relatively rare.

FRUITY: Can be due to overfermentation and/or bacterial infection before firing. An overripe taste.

FULL: A good combination of strength and color.

GONE OFF: A flat or old tea. Often denotes a high moisture content.

GREEN: An immature, "raw" character. Often due to underfermentation (sometimes underwithering).

HARD: A very pungent liquor.

HARSH: A taste generally due to underwithered leaf. Very rough.

HEAVY: A thick, strong and colory liquor with limited briskness.

HIGH-FIRED: Over-fired but not bakey or burned.

LACKING: Describes a neutral liquor. No body or pronounced characteristics.

LIGHT: Lacking strength and depth of color.

MALTY: Desirable character in some Assam teas. A full, bright tea with a taste of malt.

MATURE: Not bitter or flat.

METALLIC: A sharp coppery flavor.

MUDDY: A dull, opaque liquor.

MUSCATEL: Desirable character in Darjeeling teas. A grapey taste.

MUSTY: Suspicion of mold.

PLAIN: A liquor that is "clean" but lacking in desirable characteristics.

POINT: A bright, acidic and penetrating characteristic.

PUNGENT: Astringent with a good combination of briskness, brightness and strength (usually refers to best-quality North India teas).

QUALITY: Refers to "cup quality" and denotes a combination of the most desirable liquoring qualities.

RASPING: A very coarse and harsh liquor.

RAW: A bitter, unpleasant flavor.

SOFT: The opposite of briskness. Lacking any "live" characteristic. Caused by inefficient fermentation and/or firing.

STEWED: A soft liquor with undesirable taste. Lacks point. Caused by faulty firing at low temperatures and often insufficient air flow.

STRENGTH: Substance in cup.

SWEATY: Disagreeable taste. Poor tea.

TAINT: Characteristic or taste that is foreign to tea, such as oil, garlic, etc. Often due to being stored next to other commodities with strong characteristics of their own.

THICK: Liquor with good color and strength.

THIN: An insipid light liquor that lacks desirable characteristics.

WEEDY: A grass or hay taste related to underwithering. Sometimes referred to as "woody."

Glossary partly compiled from material kindly supplied by the British Tea Council and by T. D. Clifton of Wilson, Smithett & Co. tea brokers, London. The translator would also like to thank Kitti Cha Sangmanee for his help in researching technical terms.

BIBLIOGRAPHY

M. ASAD, *Le Chemin de La Mecque*, Fayard, Paris, 1976.

A. BARRET, *Afghanistan*, André Barret Éditeur/APC, Paris, 1989.

N. DE BLEGNY, *Le Bon Usage du thé*, Paris, 1684.

J. BLOFELD, *L'Art chinois du thé*, Dervy Livres, Paris, 1986.

A. BOUTILLY, *Le Thé, sa culture, sa manipulation*, Georges Carré et C. Naud Éditeurs, 1898.

G. BROCHARD, *Le Thé dans l'encrier*, illustrated by Ruben Alterio, Aubier, Paris, 1990.

P. BUTEL, *Histoire du thé*, Desjonquières, Paris, 1989.

K. CHOW et J. KRAEMER, *All the Tea in China*, China Books, San Francisco, 1991.

O. COUSSEMAC, *Le Thé*, Édition 2000, 1972.

P. DANN, *One for the Tea Pot*, Elm Tree Books, London, 1985.

A. DESJARDINS, *Ashrams, Grands Maîtres de l'Inde*, Albin Michel, Paris.

R. EMMERSON, *British Teapots and Tea Drinking*, HMSO, London, 1992.

M. FINKOFF, *Mes jardins de thé*, Albin Michel, Paris, 1991.

T. FOLEY, *Having Tea*, Clarkson and Potter, London, 1987.

D. M. FORREST, *A Hundred Years of Ceylon Tea*, Chatto and Windus, London, 1967.

R. FORTUNE, *A Journey to the Tea Countries*, Mildway Books, London, 1987.

A.-L. FRANKLIN, *La Vie privée d'autrefois, le Café, le Thé et le Chocolat*, Plon, Paris, 1893.

R. GIRARD et A. LAZAREFF, *Paris-sucré*, Hachette, 1990 (new edition).

J. GOODWIN, *The Gunpowder Gardens*, Chatto and Windus, London, 1990.

M. HANBURY TENSON, *The Book of Afternoon Tea*, David and Charles, London, 1980.

G. HOLT, *A Cup of Tea*, Pavilion, London.

J.-P. HOUSSAYE, *Instruction sur la manière de préparer la boisson du thé*, Paris, 1831.

J.-P. HOUSSAYE, *Monographie du thé*, Paris, 1843.

E. R. HUC, *Souvenir d'un voyage dans la Tartarie, le Tibet et la Chine pendant les années 1844, 1845, 1846*, Paris, 1849.

K. IGAGURA, *Tea Ceremony*, Hoikusha, Osaka, 1977.

J. ISLES, *A Proper Tea*, Piatkus, London, 1987.

A. ISRAEL et P. MITCHELL, *Prendre le thé*, Éditions Minerva, Paris, 1991.

J. JUMEAU-LAFOND, *Le Thé*, Nathan, Paris, 1988.

J. JUMEAU-LAFOND, S. Yi, *Le Livre de l'amateur de thé*, Laffont, Paris, 1983.

B. KETCHAM WHEATON, *L'Office et la Bouche : Histoire des mœurs et de la table en France de 1300 à 1789*, Calmann Levy, Paris, 1984.

J. V. KLAPORTH, *Voyage à Pékin à travers la Mongolie*, Paris, 1827.

M.-T. LAMBERT, *Le Thé, boisson du monde entier*, Éditions Lambert, 1982. *La Cuisine au thé*, Éditions Lambert, Paris, 1982.

T. J. LIPTON, *Leaves from the Lipton Logs*, Hutchinson and Co., 1931, and Lipton Export Limited, London, 1986.

D. R. MACGREGOR, *The Tea Clippers*, Percival Marshall, London, 1952.

C. MARONDE, *J'aime le thé*, Éditions Robert Morel, 1969 or original German edition: *Rundum den Tee*, Fischer Taschenbuch Verlag.

J. MASFIELD, *La Course du thé*, Plon, Paris, 1939.

F. MASSIALOT, *Nouvelle Instruction pour les confitures, les liqueurs et les fruits*, Paris, 1692.

F. DE MAULDE, *Sir Thomas Lipton*, Gallimard, Paris, 1990.

J. MELOR, *This Little Tea Book*, Piatkus, London, 1988.

J. NIEUHOFF, *L'Ambassadeur de la Compagnie orientale*, Leyden, 1665.

J. NORMAN, *Tea and Tisanes*, Dorling Kindersley, London, 1989.

OKAKURA, K., *The Book of Tea*, Dover Publications, New York, 1964.

M. PATTEN, *The Complete Book of Tea*, Piatkus, London, 1989.

J. PETTIGREW, *Tea Time*, Le Chêne, Paris, 1987.

H. PRASAD SHASTRI, *Écho spirituel du Japon*, Dervy Livres, Paris, 1985.

PURILLA, KINCHIN, *Tea and Taste: The Glasgow Tea Rooms, 1875-1975*, White Cockade, Oxon, 1991.

B. RAISON, *L'Empire des objets*, Du May, Paris, 1989.

R. K. RENFORD, *The Non-Official British in India to 1920*, Oxford University Press, London, 1987.

J. RUNNER, *Le Thé*, PUF, Paris, 1974.

M. SCHIAFFINO, *L'Heure du thé*, Gentleman Éditeur, Paris, 1987.

H. SIMPSON, *The London Ritz Book of Afternoon Tea*, Ebury Press, London, 1987.

M. SMITH, *Afternoon Tea*, Macmillan, London, 1986.

S. SOSHITSU, *Vie du thé, esprit du thé*, Jean-Cyrille Godefroy, 1982.

P. SYLVESTRE-DUFOUR, *Traités nouveaux et curieux du café, du thé et du chocolat*, Lyon, 1865.

S. TWININGS, *Two Hundred and Fifty Years of Tea and Coffee, 1706-1956*, Twinings, London, 1956.

W. UCKERS, *All About Tea*, New York Tea and Trade Journal Company, 1935.

J. WEATHERSTONE, *The Pioneers, 1825-1900*, Quiller Press, London, 1986.

A. WHIPPLE, *Les Clippers*, Time-Life, 1980.

R. WOLF, *Le Goût du Japon*, Flammarion, Paris, 1987. *Le Goût de la Chine*, Flammarion, Paris, 1989.

INDEX

This book is dedicated to the memory of Jane Grigson, who was to have collaborated on this project,
in grateful acknowledgment of the talent and advice she so generously offered us.

ACKNOWLEDGMENTS

The publisher and authors would like to express their special indebtedness to Mr. Kitti Cha Sangmanee of Mariage Frères, Paris, for the invaluable information that he provided throughout the preparation of this book. The chapters on "Tea Gardens" and "The Taste of Tea," in particular, would not have been possible without his help. Grateful acknowledgments are also due everyone at Mariage Frères who made it possible to photograph the tea liquors pictured on page 206, and who carefully selected the dry teas photographed on pages 230 to 237. They also deserve thanks for having helped to compile the glossary and for lending valuable objects from the Mariage Frères Tea Museum, including the tea chests pictured on pages 21, 57, 101 and 197 and the tea containers on pages 72, 199, 207, 217, 221, and 228. The authors would also like to thank Mr. Didier Jumeau-Lafond of Betjeman and Barton, as well as Ms. Mihoko Tsutsumi of the Urasenke Foundation in Paris for her helpful information on the tea ceremony.

We are also grateful to Valérie Barac'h for diligently tracking down documents, to Mr. S. H. G. Twining, London, to Anita Crocker of the British Tea Council, and to Mr. Peter Abel of the International Tea Committee, London.

Thanks also to Emmanuelle Rendu, Gilles Paris and Egert Schröder.

Finally, the publisher would like thank all those who generously supplied documents, maps and photographs, notably Maud Arqué, Terence Conran, Claude Frioux, Kari Haavisto, Grace Kirschenbaum, Lothar Menne, Olivier Scala at the Comité Français du Thé, Spink and Son, Helen Sudell, the Stylograph Agency, and Colin Webb, as well as Julie Gaskill for copyediting the English edition, and Charles Pierce for the recipe adaptation.

……他就開始試嘗百草。當他嘗到一種植物的葉子時，發現這種綠葉真奇怪，從下到上，到處流動洗滌，好似把腸胃洗滌得干干淨淨，他就稱這綠葉為「查」。以後人們叫成「茶」了。神農成年累月地爬山涉水，一種植物一樣，從春秋到利用，需要經過一段漫長的歲月。當原始人類發現茶葉對人體有醫療效用以後，對茶葉就開始注意和重視起來。據古籍記載，茶葉最初只作為藥用。到了春秋時代，已經提到用茶葉作羹飲，但沒有發展成為日常飲料的記錄。

茶和其他發現乳白色花朵的樹上的嫩葉時……

對茶葉的起源和歷史，各說紛紜，而有許多文獻的記述。有的人認為「秦人取荼」（四川），而即產茶和飲之事」，有的人根據三國孫皓以四大臣韋曜酒量太小，曾在宴會上密賜茶荈代酒，於是有人認為荼始於三國，滋味播九區》之句，有「芳荼（茶字古作荼）冠六清，溢味播九區」的句子。蔓茗荈都，翠葉青黃」。在《趙飛燕別傳》中，有一段關於漢代飲茶的記載：漢成帝崩，后（即趙飛燕）夢中見帝，帝自云中賜吾坐，帝命進茶。左右奏帝，后向日待帝不謹，不合啜此茶。

作者說飲茶的時間，至西漢時代，飲茶傳播地區逐漸廣闊。在春秋戰國後期及西漢初年，曾發生過幾次大規模的戰爭。造成了人口的大遷徙。特別是秦統一中國以後，促進了經濟和文化的交流。在唐代，南北加工及飲用方法，開始向當時的經濟、政治、文化中心陝西、河南等地傳播，這是陝西、河南成為北方古老茶區的原因。同時，蔓茗荈都，翠葉青黃。

對茶葉由藥而轉為珍貴的貢品，前後相距竟達千餘年之久。其實，我國飲茶始於飲之時間，以上各說法，前後相距竟反映在西漢時期，茶已成為皇室中的一種飲料了。又據史料記載，漢王……

江臨海蓋竹山有仙翁茶園，漢朝名士浙江余姚人虞洪，曾入山採茗，遇仙人丹丘子。浙江一帶，已有茶樹栽植，並曾採茗，遇仙人丹丘子。

明當時在江蘇、浙江一帶，已有茶樹栽培和製茶的技藝。如果沒有過去長期積累下來的茶樹栽培和製茶經驗，如果開始招收學童，傳授生產茶葉的技藝……

有人民群眾積累下來的茶葉的消費需求，哪裏能夠「課童」呢？可以想見，我國江南一帶，早在漢代飲茶就相當普遍了。在西晉以前，中國廣大地區還是把茶葉作為一種比較珍貴的飲料。到了兩晉、南北朝，產茶漸多，飲茶日益增多，據《晉書》記載：敦煌人單道開坐禪，不畏寒暑，晝夜不臥，每日吞服幾粒小石子一樣的丸藥，一種比較珍貴的飲料。

此外，只有「松蜜薑桂茯苓之氣」，似乎是蒙古人運用在選用的固形牛奶，混合以松子、桂皮、蜂蜜、薑、茯苓等而成的，飲茶蘇（又稱茶蘇）二升」。《廣陵耆中提到：「市人竟賣」。《晉南諸書》記載，往市粥之，市人竟賣」。《晉老姥每日擎一器名，往市粥之，市人竟賣，從……

葛玄曾植茶於此。浙江余姚人虞洪，上山特風味，也很快染上飲茶的嗜好。茶逐漸成為他們日常生活中不可缺少的必需品。據唐朝李肇著的《國史補》記載：唐朝有使者唐蒙之過，到了西番。烹茶帳中，常魯公說：「滌煩療渴的所謂茶。」賢普說，我這裏也有，於是叫人拿出來指着說：「此壽州者，此舒州者，此顧渚者，此新門者，此昌明者，此湖者……」可見唐時飲茶風氣之盛，西藏一帶的王公貴族家裏都已貯備各色名茶了，是同文成公主了。

中興書：有一段吳興與太守陸納生活儉樸，以茶果待客的故事……陸納為吳興太守時，衛將軍謝安欲詣納，納所設唯茶果而已。私蓄十數人饌，安既至，納所備唯茶果而已。

唐太宗的宗女文成公主，一是尼泊爾輸入西藏，文化與飲茶的風氣從內地輸入西藏，導致以後在西藏喇嘛寺中盛大茶會的出現。唐代飲茶風行，土番的松贊干布與唐朝和親，績分不開的。吐蕃的松贊干布娶有兩個王妃，是尼泊爾王女，一是唐太宗的宗女文成公主。文成公主進一步結合，導致以後在西藏喇嘛寺……

陸羽是西漢時期四川資中的一位儒生，到他亡友的妻子楊惠家裏，形影相隨，因而成了一種契約）《買賣奴隸的故事。王褒是西漢時期四川資中的一位儒生，寄居在他亡友的妻子楊惠家裏，成了一種契約。王褒的《僮約》中規定便了每天事務役，其中涉及有值的茶業。在《僮約》中規定便了去打酒，成為王褒專用的家僮，所立契約就是王褒所寫的《僮約》。

顧渚為吳興與宜興太守時，衛將軍謝安欲詣陸納，陸羽是西漢時期四川彭山縣東，距彭山縣約十餘里，為漢代經濟、文化的中心城市之一，附近吳洗滌、整理，就是規定便定了要到武陽去買茶。「武陽買茶」、「烹茶盡具」兩句。武陽即今四川彭山縣東，距彭……

《僮約》云：「汲江煮茶」……「武陽買茶」，《僮約》中「烹茶盡具」、「武陽買茶」兩句，記載了要到古代的產茶區。「武陽買茶」，就是規定便定了要到武陽和盛產茶的地方去買茶。從以上史料看，隨着茶葉生產的……

便擅斷在晉朝時茶葉由藥用而轉為飲料。以上各說法，前後相距達一兩千餘年。

山東、河北的部份地區，直至當時的首都長安，「城市多開店舖，煎茶賣之，不問道俗，投錢取飲，其茶自江淮而來，舟車相繼，所在山積，色額甚多。」同書又說：「……古人亦飲茶耳，但不如今人殢之甚，窮日盡夜，殆成風俗，始自中地，流於塞外，朝，大驅名馬市茶而歸……」可知唐時飲茶之風，已由南方傳播到黃河北岸，紛慕名而至，都從中國販運茶葉。一六六二年，嗜好茶的葡萄牙凱瑟琳公主嫁給英皇查理二世以後，朝廷中風行的葡萄酒、燒酒等烈性飲料也被以，茶消費量最多的茶客，英國成為界上最大的茶客。

茶，並本國上層社會把飲茶列為最初提到我國茶葉的是明世宗嘉靖二十八年（公元一五五九年）威尼斯著名作家拉慕修所著的《中國茶》和《海與旅行記》兩書。葡萄牙傳教士克羅茲神父是把中國茶的傳播及天主教的第一人，一五六〇年將中國茶品類及飲茶方法等知識介傳入歐洲。

後東茶，並本國上層社會把飲茶……

茶的起源、歷史、栽培、採製、煮茶、用書中對茶的起源、歷史、栽培、採製、煮茶、用茶葉，並本國上層社會把飲茶列為……

荷蘭和法國人轉少傳入的。但最初的品種及飲茶方法。以後，茶葉的英文名稱拼為 Te 而把茶的英文名稱拼為 Tea。以後端典、丹麥、法國、德國、匈牙利等國的商船紛紛慕名而至，都從中國販運茶葉。英國一個名叫龍喬茶的荷英人在廈門設立茶務機構，專門販賣茶，以廈門人讀稱發音為 Te 而把茶的英文名稱拼為 Tea。以後荷蘭人的宣傳，飲茶之風波及到英、法諸國，六三七年，荷蘭海船首次直接從中國購運大量茶葉，這是荷蘭人最時髦的飲料。一六四四年英人在廈門設立商務機構，運轉運到美洲殖民地。一六六二年，嗜好茶的葡萄牙凱瑟琳公主嫁給英皇查理二世以後，三十五年（公元一六〇七年）荷蘭船首次從澳門運往爪哇，這是最早的記錄。以後，茶葉成為荷蘭最時髦的飲料。

他就開始試嚐百草。當他嚐到這種綠葉，好似開着乳白色花朵的樹上的嫩葉時，發現這種綠葉葉真奇怪，一吃到肚子裡，就從上到下，到處流動洗滌，好似把腸胃洗滌得干干淨淨，他就稱這種綠葉為「查」。以後人們就把腸胃洗滌得干干淨淨，全靠茶來解救。茶和其他植物一樣，從發現到利用，每天都得中毒幾次，全靠茶來解救。茶和其他植物一樣，從發現到重視，需要經過一段漫長的歲月。到了春秋時代，已經提到用茶葉作饌飲，但沒有專用作為飲料的記錄。

到了春秋時代，已經提到用茶葉作饌飲，對茶葉開始注意和重視起來。茶和其他加工及飲用方法，開始向當時的經濟、政治、文化中心陝西、河南等地傳播，這是陝西、四川、雲南一帶的茶樹栽培、茶葉加工及飲用方法，開始向當時的經濟、政治、文化中心陝西、河南成為北方古老茶區的原因。同時，傳播。

茶的起源和利用的歷史了。因此，對茶飲的年代，無論記載是更不消說或是春秋，都說得太遲，更不消說是在晉代了。根據記載，周武王伐紂後，巴蜀等西南小國曾以所產的茶葉作「貢品」呢？可以想見，我國江南一帶早在漢代，中國廣大地區還是把茶葉作為一種比較珍貴的飲料的。

時間，至西漢時代，飲茶傳播地區逐漸廣闊。在春秋戰國後期及西漢初年，曾發生過幾次大規模的戰爭，造成了人口的大遷徙。特別是秦統一中國以後，促進了經濟和文化的交流，開始向當時的經濟、政治、文化中心陝西、河南等地傳播，這是陝西、四川、雲南一帶的茶樹栽培、茶葉加工及飲用方法。

後東來，從最初提到我國茶葉的是明世紀宗嘉靖三十八年（公元一五五九年）威尼斯著名作家拉馬司沃氏所著的《中國茶》和《海與旅行記》兩書。葡萄牙傳教士克羅茲神父是在中國傳播天主教的第一人。一五六○年將中國茶品類及飲茶方法等知識傳入歐洲。